Homilies KIDS CAN SEE

Msgr. Dermot R. Brennan

Our Sunday Visitor Publishing Division
Our Sunday Visitor, Inc.
Huntington, Indiana 46750

Nihil Obstat:
Rev. Michael Heintz
Censor Librorum
Imprimatur:
✠ John M. D'Arcy
Bishop of Fort Wayne-South Bend
January 5, 2002

Scripture citations, unless otherwise noted, are from the *New American Bible With Revised New Testament*, copyright © 1986, 1970 by the Confraternity of Christian Doctrine, Inc. All rights reserved. Every reasonable effort has been made to determine copyright holders and to secure permissions as needed. If any copyrighted materials have been inadvertently used without proper credit being given in one manner or another, please notify Our Sunday Visitor in writing so that future editions may be corrected accordingly.

Our Sunday Visitor Publishing Division
Our Sunday Visitor, Inc.
200 Noll Plaza
Huntington, IN 46750

ISBN: 1-931709-04-1 (Inventory No. T8)
LCCCN: 2002101152

Cover design by Monica Haneline
Cover photo by John Zierten
Interior design by Sherri L. Hoffman
Interior art by Kevin Davidson

PRINTED IN THE UNITED STATES OF AMERICA

I dedicate the homilies in this book to you — priests, deacons, catechists, and schoolteachers — who want so much to bring to the children the Good News that is Jesus, in the hope that you will not only benefit from my ideas but, more importantly, will be further inspired to develop your own.

Table of Contents

III. CHURCH TEACHINGS

Introduction

Frequently when I have the opportunity to speak to young people, I mention that they are often referred to as "the Future of the Church" or "the Hope of the Church" or "the Church of Tomorrow." I then express the opinion that they are not "the Church of Tomorrow" but the Church of *Today*. They're younger or smaller than most other Catholics, but they are just as important as anyone else. That's not just to make them feel good about themselves. It's the truth! They are just as vital to the life of the Church as anyone else in it. "Unless you . . . become like children, you will not enter the kingdom of heaven" (Mt 18:3).

Yet, whenever we are called upon to speak to the children, we either "toss a few thoughts together" (probably thoughts they have heard from us several times already!) or we immediately fall into a state of panic and ask ourselves four questions: What will I say? How can I get them to listen? How can I hold their attention? *Whom can I get to take my place?*

This book is an attempt to provide the answers to the first three questions — and eliminate the fourth — in the hope that the reader will gradually develop a comfort zone where speaking to children is concerned. Further, if my goal is truly reached, readers will develop a degree of confidence in their *own* creative instincts that will lead them to work out some of their own ideas, approaches, props, and illustrations for use in speaking to children. I believe firmly that God gives us far more talents than we acknowledge; and yet, in this world that worships professionalism, we feel that unless we are outstanding, we shouldn't try things at all. I hope you will feel differently after working with some of my examples and then developing ideas of your own.

How does this book differ from many of those already on the market? Essentially, it will offer suggestions and methods for using visual/audio aids to hold the children's attention and get across a lesson, and not just provide stories ("Tabernacle Talks for Tots," we used to call them!).

It will provide specific directions about how to make these visuals so that anyone who can print, cut, paste, and is willing to shop for odd things — or who can find someone willing to do these things for him — can produce everything in this volume. The homilies in this book are not just "ideas." They've all been done at one or more Masses, so I know they work.

It took me a long time (*too* long) to learn that merely speaking to children, especially those of preschool age through second grade, would hardly hold their attention. Even then, I gradually came to understand that, in a classroom setting, they learned far more from coloring a picture in a workbook or singing a song with a message than they did from my "super profound" words, no matter how hard I tried to make them appealing to the children.

Yes, my words were an important component of the lesson because I never taught a song without first going over the words and the lesson they taught, or had the children color without first talking about the picture. But it gradually became clear that nothing locked the message into their hearts better than the singing or the coloring.

Transferring that hard-learned lesson to the homily, I concluded that children are influenced much more by pictures than by words (as the old adage said about a picture being worth a thousand words, but who was listening?). So I set out to try to develop homilies for our monthly Family Mass — where the emphasis is on the little ones — that would not only hold children's attention but also teach them the lesson I wanted them to learn.

In the process, I discovered several things.

First of all, it is not easy to do. We all have been trained to be far too cerebral, far too verbal. This may work with well-educated adults, but it goes nowhere with little children — and perhaps nowhere with some big children, too. I found myself spending far more time planning a homily for the Children's Mass than for any of the other Masses I celebrate each weekend.

Secondly, the real difficulty is in finding in the Scripture passages some valid application to the child's life and then developing a pictorial way to get that across. That's where the time is spent: revving up a frequently underused imagination and brainstorming with the Lectionary readings in hand. Once the message is determined, then we have to get the creative juices really flowing, and so the search for ideas for illustrating the message can begin.

The most important ingredient in this process is *prayer*. No, not the prayer of desperation we sometimes offer when ideas won't come, but prayer to the Holy Spirit to give us the ideas *He* intends the children to receive that Sunday. After all, it is His Scripture passage and His message that we are trying to get across. So quiet time, usually in the church or chapel, is a sine qua non for working these things out.

One of the real bonuses I have received from this experience is that whenever I feel that the material I have worked out after such prayer is not everything I want it to be, that's when it seems to go over the best. (Could it be that when they are the *Holy Spirit's* ideas, they work better than when they are mine?)

Two rewards flow from this process.

The first is the look of rapture that can come over the children's faces as you draw them more and more into your presentation and the message of Jesus. I perform magic as a hobby and have often said that I wish everyone could have the experience of seeing children's eyes light up and hearing their laughter and wonderment as a trick unfolds. Well, that same experience can be yours with a well-planned and properly carried-out children's homily. It takes work, of course, but doesn't everything that is worthwhile?

The second reward comes from the parents. Not only are they grateful that you bothered to make a special effort to convey the faith to their children, but they often comment that they, too, benefited much from the homily. (The only time I take exception to that comment is when they express the wish that *every* homily be a children's homily. That scares me, not only because of the preparatory work involved but also because of the expressed level of their faith!) Sometimes they will tell you that the homily was the principal topic of family conversation on the way home or at the breakfast table, and then you *know* that you have scored one for the Holy Spirit — and isn't that what giving a homily is all about?

Remember to let humor just happen spontaneously in response to what the children say. During the homily on Christ the King Sunday, I asked, "What do kings do?" and one young girl answered, "They [i.e., kings] boss people around and tell them what to do." The adults laughed, and I added, "And that's why they don't let women become kings!"

Delivered with a smile and a laugh, that kind of line can go a long way to draw the parents in, so don't be afraid to capitalize on a youngster's line. However, delivering it in the wrong way, you can lose half the crowd — the female half! So be careful and learn to edit your responses in the split second you have before you deliver them. *If there is any sense at all that a line will not be well received, don't use it!* It's not worth the risk. Never try to be funny just for the purpose of being funny. Let the humor come from the children. For example, when I later asked, "What does a king need?" the same little girl answered, "He needs a queen!" — a great line that I did not try to top!

So, if you are ready to let your hair down a bit and get out the construction paper, poster board, foam core, paste, scissors, Scotch tape, and a few other items I will explain as we go along, then let's get started. And may the cobwebs fall away from your imagination, your long-hidden artistic talents finally show forth, your desk (or floor) begin to look like that of a kindergarten teacher, and the sights and sounds of children enjoying themselves (yes, even in church!) surround you next Sunday morning.

Some Preliminary Ideas

1. Let's begin with a basic principle when speaking to children: **Always speak so the youngest can understand; the older ones will have no difficulty.**

    I strongly suggest that you *not* deliver these homilies from the ambo, or pulpit, which usually is located off to the side of the sanctuary, providing poor sight-lines for showing the props. The small space is also restrictive, and the lectern serves as a barrier between you and the children. Instead, step out onto the predella and move around. This brings you closer to the children and enables to you establish real contact with them. It also gives a sense of freedom not usually felt in the pulpit.

2. Try to have the children come up to the sanctuary area and sit on the floor in front of you. They are used to doing that in the lower grades and at home, and it makes them more relaxed and spontaneous than if they stay in their seats. (That's too much like school.) You will find it much easier to speak to them in this setting, and it also makes them feel very special! You can also use the moments it takes for them to assemble to bring your props into view and, conversely, to put them away as the children return to their seats at the end of the homily.

3. If you can possibly purchase a wireless microphone system for use at these Masses (a clip-on, *not* handheld), you will find it will pay enormous dividends. It allows you to walk about freely, to have both hands free (for making gestures and holding props), while guaranteeing that everyone in the church will hear you. You will also find it increasingly useful as you celebrate other liturgies, especially on special holidays such as Palm Sunday, the Triduum, Christmas (for the Nativity Proclamation and/or the Blessing of the Crèche), and other occasions. And please don't buy a cheap one! If the homily is the one time we are in direct contact with the vast majority of our people, let's use every means at our command, electronic or otherwise, to maximize the opportunity. So go for really good sound — digital if possible. But please stay away from those tinny-sounding, cheap wireless mikes sold in some of the electron-

ics stores. If they don't produce a pleasant sound, they serve only to distract from what you're saying.

4. Finally, I am very much aware that many of you don't draw well, have poor handwriting, are not skilled at cutting and pasting, don't go shopping in toy stores, and rarely get involved in doing any arts and crafts. *Don't let that stop you!* There are many people in your parish who are good at these things and would be delighted to help provide the props you need for these homilies. *Get them involved!* They are eager to lend their talents to the cause of the Church and will be thrilled to see their handiwork displayed in a very important task — that of bringing children and their families closer to God. Just be sure you acknowledge their contribution at the end of the homily. That's really all the "reward" they will want. *(Note: Many illustrations have been provided for the reader's use. These can be either enlarged on photocopiers or, if too small for that, used as templates.)*

SECTION I

SACRAMENTS

The Lottery

(Baptism, Church, Gifts and Graces, Salvation History)

This homily was fashioned for use at Camp Marist in New Hampshire, where I have spent my summer vacation for the past 37 years. The challenge at the camp is to engage the entire enrollment (290 boys, ages 6 to 15) at a Sunday morning Mass – and remembering that often the camp is trilingual! Yes, there are boys there from the United States who speak English, from Canada who speak French, and from several Latino countries who speak Spanish. How does one reach such a mixed group? By keeping them involved through participation while making the presentation as simple as possible. (Toward the end of the homily, I ran into a problem because of the languages – a problem I will refer to later on – but one that you probably will not have to deal with. However, this presentation has proven itself, allowing extensive involvement of listeners.)

PROPS

- As many small pay envelopes (2 1/2" x 4") or inexpensive letter envelopes as there are children in attendance.
- Slips of paper – one for each envelope – on which are printed the letters/numerals "**132JCDR7S4U**." Insert one slip of paper into each envelope and seal it. The envelopes are then numbered in sequence on the outside.
- A bowl with slips of paper bearing the same numbers that are on the outside of the envelopes.
- A card (approximately 22" x 8") with the same "132JCDR7S4U" printed large enough for all to see when you hold it up.
- Some kind of inexpensive prize given to the winner of the initial raffle.

The goal of this homily is to teach the children about the extraordinary goodness of God to each one of us as revealed in the person and life of Jesus; therefore, it can be used with any text that teaches this lesson.

The envelopes are passed out to the children (one for each child) as they enter the church. They are to put the envelope in a pocket or in the hymnbook rack in front of them until it is used.

At the proper time, ask each child to take his/her envelope and look at the number on the front; then show them the prize. (I use a large manila envelope marked "**BIG BUCKS**," in which there are several of those giant-sized $10 or $20 bills available in joke or fun shops. I have also used a very large candy bar.)

Whatever the prize, simply bring into view the bowl containing the numbered slips of paper and ask a child to come forward and pick a number from the bowl. Before reading the winning number, tell the children that you want the winner to stand up and call out: "I win! I win!" Then read the winning number, wait to hear "I win! I win!" and call the winner forward to receive the prize.

The purpose of this initial raffle is to establish the whole notion of a raffle or lottery and to have the children hear one of their own call out, "I win! I win!" (You will see the importance of this later.)

Now call the children's attention to the fact that the envelopes they hold are sealed. Tell them *not to open them until you say so.* Then talk about the lottery — they should all know what a lottery is: a raffle for a really *big prize.* (We set that up with the raffle just held.) Say also that lottery numbers are usually long, and that each of their envelopes contains a piece of paper with a long lottery number on it. Emphasize that you will read the winning number, and that they must be quiet so that they can hear every letter and numeral. Finally, tell them that the person with the winning number *must* stand up and call out, "I win! I win!" — or otherwise the prize will not be awarded. Now tell them to open their envelopes, take out the slip inside, and listen carefully.

Take up the large card with the winning number "132JCDR7S4U" printed on it, making sure the number is facing you so that they can't see it. Read off the numbers and letters, one at a time, pausing between each letter/numeral in order to build suspense. You will actually hear the children getting more excited as you get closer to the end of the number. Naturally, when you get to the last letter "U," *every* child in the gathering will stand up and shout, "I win! I win!" — and that's the secret to the whole device: *Each child is a winner!* What does all this mean?

The answer is in the winning number, and you can develop this at the pace you sense will work at the time.

The rest of the homily is spent showing how every baptized person is a winner, because baptism opens the way to all sorts of wonderful gifts from God. Then explain the winning number:

"**1**" tells us there is *one* God.

"**3**" tells us there are *three* Persons in that one God.

"**2**" tells us that the *Second* Person of the Trinity, the Son of God, became man, and that His name is "**JC**" — *Jesus Christ*.

"**D**" tells us that He *died* on the cross to take away our sins.

"**R**" tells us He *rose* again to give us the hope of eternal life in heaven.

"**7**" tells us that Jesus continues to be with us in the *seven* sacraments ("**S**"), and

"**4U**" tells the children He did it all "*for you*"!

As mentioned, you can develop each of these points to the degree you wish or simply leave the children with the general concept of how much God loves us. You can also say that none of this is automatic; we have to follow Jesus and His Church if we want to share in all He has promised. Just like the lottery, "You have to be in it to win it!"

(By the way, the language problem I mentioned earlier came with the "4U." It makes a fine rebus for English-speaking children — and kids love puns and word games — but it was quite difficult for the translators to get across the idea of this one to the French- and Spanish-speaking children.)

I realize this homily takes some time to prepare, but this is another instance when you can involve members of your Children's Liturgy Committee in making the necessary preparations. You will find it worth your while since the process gets every single child involved in the homily — at least until the lottery is over!

Finally, the same idea can be used with other teachings, as long as you can figure out a winning "lottery number" or anagram to suit the teaching you choose.

You Are the Prophet!

(Baptism, Confirmation, Witnessing, John the Baptist)

One of the primary effects of our being baptized is that immediately after the water is poured on our head, the priest anoints us with the special oil we call *chrism*. As he rubs this oil on our head, he declares that we are anointed priest, prophet, and king. This is a fact little referred to, yet all three roles are important to our Catholic life. We become sharers in the priesthood of Christ as members of the worshiping community. We follow Christ our King as He leads us to the kingdom of heaven. And along the way, under God's grace, we have the power to choose the way we will go; so we are, in a sense, king or ruler over our own lives.

Our role of *prophet* is the object of this homily.

PROPS

When I first developed this homily, there was only one prop: a picture of an old prophet. However, after giving it once or twice, I decided to expand on it and added two more pictures: one of a contemporary boy and one of a contemporary girl. This may necessitate asking for help from someone in your parish who loves to draw. You need to draw (or have drawn) a picture of a prophet on a large sheet of poster board (22" x 28"). It should show just the head and shoulders and should be of a man who is old and with a long white beard (i.e., the traditional image we all have of prophets). It must be carefully drawn so that the face, when cut out in an oval (much like those images we stand behind for comedy photographs at amusement parks), will fit the size of an adult's head — *yours!* The face part is held in place by a couple of pieces of masking tape so that the oval can be easily removed when it is time for you to look through it. (Unless you can find the kind that does not stick permanently, Scotch tape holds too well and will tear the poster board as you remove it. You might also try some lightweight press-on Velcro strips.) You may also want to reinforce

PROPHET

the side of the picture with heavy cardboard so that the picture won't flop back and forth as you and the children hold it in front of yourselves. Another suggestion would be to use foam core instead of poster board, but you will need a very sharp instrument to cut out the oval (I have used the small saw on a Leatherman tool).

As stated above, the other two pictures should be of a contemporary boy and girl in order to show that *they* are today's prophets. The construction would be the same as for the older prophet, except that the hole where the face will show should be a bit smaller so as to accommodate the face of a child. (See illustrations.)

The three pictures should be lying facedown, side by side on a table or on the altar until you want the children to see them. If you display them too soon, they could easily distract the children from your opening words and cause them to miss the message.

HOMILY

Begin by saying that just as the prophets of old were anointed with oil to show they were prophets, so we are also anointed at our baptism, right after the priest or deacon pours the water on our head. As a result, everyone who is here today who was baptized is a prophet!

But what exactly is a prophet? He is *not* someone who foretells the future, although we almost always use the term in that way. Indeed, in many instances when the prophets made statements that were later fulfilled in either the Old or New Testament, they were not aware of what they were foretelling. It is only when we look back that we can say, "That was foretold by Isaiah!" or by one of the other prophets.

What, then, is the role of the prophet? It is *to speak for God.* We are to tell other people what God wants us all to do, and then we must *show* them by doing it ourselves.

Here you show them the picture of the old prophet. Speak for a moment or two to review the role the prophets were called to play (i.e., not to predict the future, but to speak for God). Then recall that *you* were called to be a prophet when you were baptized. Then remove the masking tape from the back of the picture of the old prophet, and the oval will come away with it. Now you can hold the picture in front of you so that your face will appear in the hole. You thereby are pictured as a prophet as we so often depict one.

In this position, speak to the children about how you are a prophet every time you teach them about God and how He wants us to act, whether you are preaching at Mass, teaching them in the school or CCD program, or whenever. So just as the prophets of old spoke for God, you are called to speak for God in today's world as a priest.

However — and this is **very** important — you became a prophet a long time before you became a priest. It happened when you were baptized! That means everyone here today who has been baptized has been called by God to be a prophet, too!

Here you ask for a boy and a girl (preferably no younger than fourth or fifth grade) to join you. As they approach the altar, pick up the picture of the boy, show it to everyone, and hand it to the young volunteer. Do the same with the picture of the girl. Then ask each of them to remove the face-oval from the picture (you may have to assist them with this) and to hold the picture so that his/her face shows through the hole.

Now it is time for them to act as prophets, so you announce that you will ask them questions, to which they are to give the answers they think a prophet should give.

(Note: This is one of the few homilies in this book that will benefit from preparing the "volunteers." Try to have a brief meeting with the boy and girl *before the homily, to go over the questions you will ask. It's only fair that they be helped with the answers, especially if they are fairly young.)*

When I use this homily, it is often to provide answers to moral questions that children face every day. For example, after one of the children has assumed the position of prophet by holding the picture up so that he/she can see through it, you might ask, "Suppose someone in school asks you to give the answer to a question on a test. What do you think God's prophet would say to that person?" Or, "Suppose some other child borrowed one of your toys and then, by accident, broke it. What do you think God's prophet would say to that child?" Or, "Suppose someone asked if you had done something you were not supposed to do, and you were tempted to tell a lie so as not to be punished. What do you think God's prophet would say to you?"

Similar questions and answers can be used according to the children to whom you are speaking. If this is at a School Mass, you might confer with the principal or teachers to see if there are any issues that *they* would like you to deal with! (I have even used this device with middle-schoolers and those preparing for confirmation, to emphasize their future role as witnesses to Jesus and their faith.)

The purpose of this homily, then, is to teach the children (and their parents!) that God has shown us the way we are to live if we want to please Him, and we are likewise to show that way to others. It is in telling and showing others the way to God that we use our power as prophets.

It can also be used at special times such as Christmas and Holy Week/Easter with older children to test them on the many aspects of both great events that were foretold by the Old Testament prophets. This approach, which plays into the usual understanding of a prophet as one who foretells the future, is used in a more didactic teaching setting. This also illustrates how such a prop can be used in more than one way.

We have shown that girls as well as boys can be prophets; it has nothing to do with age or gender. This can be clearly shown by the fact that, although the "old man" image is one we all seem to have, the Scriptures show us that the prophets were of different ages (mention Jeremiah and John the Baptist as examples), and there were also prophetesses mentioned in both the Old Testament and the New Testament (Deborah and Anna, for example). *The main point* is that *all* of us — boys and girls, men and women — are anointed prophets and are thereby chosen by God to speak for Him both in word and in action.

Little Things Are Important

(Eucharist, First Communion, Humility, Value of a Child)

In response to a desperate call from a priest friend who phoned the night before First Communion in his parish asking for help with a suitable homily, I decided I was entitled to needle him a bit in return for my help. I asked, "Did you buy the book?" He said, "Yes, I did, but I don't have time to read through it now. Help!" I told him to call back in a few minutes and I would try to have something for him. There was no time for him to buy the props necessary for my favorite First Communion homily (it's the next one in this book), so I put together a homily using readily accessible props. Since then I have used it myself to speak about the Real Presence to children, even up to the seventh grade.

PROPS

- A Walkman with headphones, a cassette, and one battery.
- A deck of cards or a set of checkers.
- A puzzle from which you remove one piece.
- A small purse (a rosary case will do) containing 99 cents.

With a marking pen, write "**$1.00**" on the back of the puzzle in large numbers.

These items should all be in a box or gift bag so that they can be shown one at a time. At the bottom of the bag or box, you should also have a small host and a cruet of wine.

HOMILY

Begin by stating that "*Little things are important.*" Then demonstrate this using the props assembled. Show the Walkman, complete with earphones and a cassette, which you insert. You wonder why it is not playing and then check the battery compartment, only to find that there is only *one* battery in it. Because you don't have that one more little battery, the rest of the equipment is useless. *Little things are important.*

Now remove the deck of cards from the box, show them to the children, and ask how many cards there should be in the deck. The children will answer, "Fifty-two." Take a card out and toss it aside, stating that although there is only one card missing, the other 51 are useless for a card game. *Little things are important.*

Show the jigsaw puzzle and point out that one piece is missing. You can't complete the puzzle without that one piece. Add the piece to show that the puzzle is now complete. *Little things are important.*

Now state that you would like to buy the puzzle, and show that the price of $1.00 is marked on the back. Take out the purse, ask one of the children to step forward (one who is old enough to add coins without a calculator!), and pour the coins into his/her hand. Ask the child to count the coins, one at a time, back into the purse as you hold it. The child will find only 99 cents. So, because you are missing one penny, you can't buy the puzzle. *Little things are important.*

Finally, show them a host and a cruet of wine, each worth only a penny or two. But in a few moments, you point out, they will become priceless because they will be changed into the Body and Blood of Jesus. This is the greatest example that *little things are important.*

From here, you should be able to bring this homily to a fitting conclusion.

This adaptation of a homily is a good example of what can be done when one brainstorms a bit. As they say today, "Think outside the box!"

Sometimes Things Are More Than They Appear

(Eucharist, First Communion, Differences in People)

This homily deals with the Holy Eucharist and is especially applicable at First Holy Communion. This mystery is the center of our faith, and in my opinion, we don't speak about it enough. Admittedly, it is not an easy concept to get across, even to adults, because, after all, we are dealing with a totally unique and invisible change of bread and wine into the Body and Blood, Soul and Divinity of Jesus. In one sense, all we can do is repeat over and over the components of the Church's teaching and fall back on our faith to accept and believe the reality. After all, during the Eucharistic Prayer, don't we proclaim "the mystery of faith"?

This presentation is one way to make the concept as visible as it can be made, and I have found that this homily has worked just as well with adults as with children. (Let's not forget that adults are as deeply touched by visuals as are children. They are just different — except in this case, since the mystery of the Eucharist is just as deep for adults as for children, maybe more so.)

This presentation depends very much on the visuals used; they actually tell the story more powerfully than the words of explanation. You will see what I mean as we go along. The props I used were all as different from one another as I could make them, except for one thing: each one had a second use — different from and perhaps more important than the first — but not immediately visible. Let me explain through examples.

PROPS

These are the ones I used:
- A wax figure of a rooster that was also a candle.
- A tile for placing hot objects on a table, but it had four little drawers for storing matches on the bottom of it.

- A child's toy that looked like a teddy bear, but with his top hat unscrewed revealing that the toy was a container for liquid, and that the top hat was a cup.
- A sick-call set in the form of a crucifix (the "old-timers" could relate to this very well).
- A flashlight that also had a siren attached to it that went off when the switch was pulled back instead of pushed forward. (The kids loved this one!)
- A rosary that looked like a beautiful necklace when only one decade was displayed in a jewelry case (the rest of the beads and the crucifix were concealed behind the cardboard displaying the single decade).
- A large host and a cruet of wine.

Please note that I did not use all of these objects in one homily — perhaps only three plus the bread and wine. But I have used each of them at some time and offer them as suggestions. You can find other such double-use items, as I did, in toy stores, hardware stores, or those fascinating swap shops! They just have to be items with two different uses — the second of which is not as visible as the first.

HOMILY

The homily should be quite evident by now. First, establish the basic theme of the homily by stating the title and then repeating it: "*Things Are Not Always Just What They Appear to Be; Sometimes They're More.*" Then offer to show the children examples of what you mean. Show each of the items, pointing out its obvious first purpose (e.g., the toy teddy bear). Then show that "this is more than it appears to be" and show the second use (e.g., the fact that the teddy bear is also a small Thermos-type container). Unscrew the hat/cup and pour the contents (milk/soda) into it. Pour the liquid back into the teddy bear container, replace the cup, and return it to the box. Continue with the other items that you have obtained, demonstrating the double use of each.

Finally, pick up the host and the cruet of wine and explain how little actual real value they now have — a mere few cents at most. Then speak of what takes place after the words of consecration are spoken: the bread becomes the Body of Jesus, and the wine becomes the Blood of Jesus. They are of *infinitely* greater value afterward than before, literally priceless. Then make whatever point you wish about the Eucharist: that the change is invisible but very, very real; that what appears to still be bread and wine is now truly the Body and Blood of Jesus; that our "Amen" spoken just before receiving Jesus means "*I believe it*"; that we receive Jesus not as a reward, but to strengthen us for the week ahead. (Perhaps challenge those who leave directly after receiving Him to be more aware of Him whom they have just received and spend more time in prayer, and so on.)

The success of this presentation depends on your own imagination and determination in locating those objects that "are not always just what they appear to be, they are *more*," and then leading those listening to a deeper realization that they are not receiving a "what" but a "WHO" when they receive Holy Communion.

As previously indicated, this can carry just as strong a message to the adults as to the children, as I have witnessed when I used it at First Communion celebrations, when whole families were present.

Additional Thought

This presentation also teaches a very important lesson in using props: **Unless it is essential for getting your lesson across, use the props early in your homily and then put them aside.** So, for example, with all the items in a tin box, I set the theme by telling the children and adults I want them to think of just one thought today: "Things are not always just what they appear to be; sometimes, they're more." Then show and demonstrate how each of the items are more than they appear to be by holding them up for all to see while you point out the double use of each. As you finish with each, put it back in the box so that it cannot be seen again. This will prevent each prop from being a continuing distraction and allow you to put the principal focus on the last two – the bread and wine – around which you base your principal message.

An Added Application

The basic idea of this homily and the props used can also find a totally different application – namely, that **people** *are not always who* *they first appear to be; sometimes they are much more.* Just as we moved from the various props selected to the bread and wine that become Jesus, so we could use the same props to move from the negative way we sometimes initially judge people to a more positive view when we find out — either from someone else who really knows them or by getting to know them better ourselves — that they are quite different from how we first saw them.

This can be applied to physical appearances, differences in ethnic origin, socioeconomic circumstances, racial stereotypes, gender differences, and so on. A presentation on any one of these themes could be introduced during the first part of this homily (using the props), even when addressing a group of adults or professional people.

It's Cleanup Time!

(Penance, Reconciliation, Lent, God's Mercy)

This homily is about the power of the Sacrament of Penance (Reconciliation) to "clean up" our soul. It involves some simple magic, holds the attention of those listening, and delivers a strong message.

PROPS

The first thing necessary is six handkerchiefs. They can be very inexpensive, but should be all the same size. If new, I suggest that you wash them to remove the stiffness. Then, using a felt-tip marker, on one write the word "**LIES**" three or four times at different angles, large enough to be seen at a distance. On the second one, write the word "**DISOBEYS**" in the same fashion, perhaps using a different color. On the third, write the word "**CURSES**," again in a different color. That leaves three clean handkerchiefs.

Obtain two paper bags (sacks) from the grocery store, or those brown bags sold in packs of 25 or 50 for use as lunch sandwich bags. All bags must be the same size. Cut one of the bags in half from top to bottom: begin at the top of one side, cut along the middle crease down to the bottom, then across the middle of the bottom and up the other side along the middle crease. You now have two half-bags. Put one aside.

Apply some paste on the sides of the half-bag. Insert the half-bag inside the remaining whole bag so that the half-bag is fastened along the sides of the *front* inside of the whole bag. The open side of the half-bag should face the front of the whole bag. In this way, you have created a bag with two compartments of equal size. Finally, using a single-edge razor blade or a sharp knife, score the front of the bag (to give it a perforated effect) so that the front can be easily torn away without destroying the whole bag. (See illustration.) If the bag is large enough, you might want to print "**ROOM OF RECONCILIATION**" on the front of it.

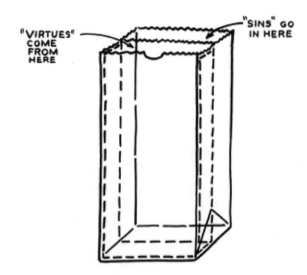

"VIRTUES" COME FROM HERE

"SINS" GO IN HERE

Now put the three clean handkerchiefs into the front compartment, one at a time (so that they can be brought out one at a time). Crumple up the other three to make them look used and soiled, and put them next to the bag.

The purpose of this homily is to show the children the power of confession, how it takes away sin, and how they get a fresh start at doing God's will. Begin by showing the three soiled handkerchiefs in a bundle. Tell them this represents their soul when it has sins on it.

Show them the first one (LIES), and talk briefly about the problems that come with lying: the person who lies displeases God and often ends up having to tell more than one lie.

Show the second handkerchief (DISOBEYS), and tell them this is usually why they have to lie! They do something wrong and then deny it or blame someone else; so, if they learn to obey, they will remove the need to lie. If they lie to impress people or to take away another person's good name, then these are two more kinds of sins we have to confess (pride and calumny).

Show the third handkerchief (CURSES), and say that most young people start cursing because they think it makes them sound tough or grown-up. Tell them that cursing is also wrong for grown-ups (another message for the adults present!). All that cursing really shows is that the person who has to use bad language doesn't know how to speak well and thinks very little of himself/herself.

(If these sins are not appropriate for the age group you are addressing, print whatever you wish on the three "sin" handkerchiefs.)

Now, pick up the bag, identify it as the "Room of Reconciliation," and proceed to drop the three soiled handkerchiefs, one at a time, into the *rear* compartment, pushing them down into it. Talk about the wonderful gift that confession is, that as long as we bring our sins to the priest — who stands in for God — and admit them, and that we promise to try not to do them again, God will take them away and even forget about them. When you have said this, reach into the *front* compartment, and one at a time, draw out the three clean handkerchiefs, showing that the sins are gone. "Now," you say, "we are able to try again, with God's grace, to be holy people."

Naturally, the children (and adults!) will want to see the inside of the bag, figuring that you merely switched one set of handkerchiefs for another (which is exactly what you did). So, while holding the back compartment closed at the top with one hand, use the other hand to tear down the front that you scored with the blade or knife. This will show the bag to be empty. Crumple it up and put it aside. (Remember to retrieve it after the homily for two reasons: [1] so the children don't discover that the soiled hankies are still in the bag and [2] so you can use the hankies another time in another homily.)

Conclude by pointing out that we are the same persons after confession that we were before, except that now our sins are gone and forgotten. God doesn't make us into someone new, because He loves us as we are. He doesn't change us into a new person. We have to do that with His grace, His help. So, if we sin again, we should go to confession and ask God to give us another chance to grow in holiness. Because He loves us, He will do just that.

If this is used for children who have not yet made their First Confession, then the lesson can be modified to have them tell God they are sorry and/or tell the person they have offended (e.g., their mother, father, teacher, brother, sister, or friend) that they are sorry. Stress that the way we show we are *really* sorry is to change and try to be better.

6

By Your Fruits You Will Be Known

(Confirmation, Living Faith, Showing Catholicism, Multipurpose Teaching Device)

B y their fruits you will know them" (Mt 7:16), one of the most popular quotations from the New Testament, presented the challenge to bring it down to a level that would be appealing to the children. This was done in a manner that proved to be quite successful, not only because of the visuals used, but also because at least a few of the children were actively involved in the actual presentation.

PROPS

The use of foam core poster material proved invaluable. It is available at most good art- or office-supply stores — and although it is more expensive than regular poster board, its rigidity allows the children to handle it and insert pushpins into it.

You will need four pieces of foam core, approximately 24" x 26". Three of the pieces show an identical picture of a tree. These can be made of poster board (green for the foliage and brown for the trunk), cut and pasted on the foam core. (See illustration.) The fourth piece shows an evergreen made the same way.

You will also need 27 cutout pieces of fruit, 9 each of 3 kinds: 9 oranges, 9 apples, and 9 clusters of cherries. For the oranges and apples, just draw 1 of each, cut it out, and use it to trace the other 8. Obviously, these should be made from orange and red poster board.

To make the cherry clusters, go to a stationery store and buy a package of round price-tag stick-ons. The stick-ons come in white or colors, so buy the red ones. Paste seven or eight of them in a cluster on a sheet of white paper, slightly overlapping one another so that they look like a cluster of cherries. (If you can only find white stick-ons, just color them red with a Magic Marker.) Now cut out the cluster around the outer edge

GREEN

GREEN

BROWN

BROWN

of the stick-ons so that none of the white paper is showing. Finally, take a felt pen and trace the outline of all the stickers that do not form the outside border of the cluster. In this way, rather than appear as just an irregular red blob, the individual circles ("cherries") can be seen.

You will need three paper plates or small trays. On each of these, place three of each of the three different fruits (each of these should have a pushpin through the top of it). So each plate or tray should have three apples, three oranges, and three cherry clusters.

You will also need eight or nine yellow discs (about 3" in diameter) cut from yellow poster board, with a pushpin in each. On these discs write these or similar words, one on each: **DAILY PRAYER, WEEKEND MASS, OBEDIENT, FORGIVING, TRUTHFUL, PATIENT, KIND WORDS, KIND DEEDS, GENEROUS**, etc. These should also be on a paper plate or small tray. For little children, you would make them age-appropriate (e.g., **OBEY, SHARE, PLAY FAIR**).

You are now ready to begin.

HOMILY

Begin by showing the three identical trees. These can be held by altar servers. The evergreen tree should not be shown yet. Point to the first and say, "This is an apple tree." Point to the second and say, "This is an orange tree." Point to the third and say, "This is a cherry tree." The children will look at you with a puzzled expression, and some will probably ask, "How can you tell?" You now have their attention! You might even repeat this sequence to heighten their curiosity as to how you can tell. Either they will tell you that there is no fruit on the trees or, if they don't (hardly likely, since children love to point out how much they know as well as call attention to mistakes made by adults), you act surprised at yourself for not having put the fruit on the trees.

Now call three children forward (those having enough dexterity to pin the fruit on the trees), and assign one to each of the trees. Then hand each of them one of the paper plates or small trays holding the nine pieces of fruit. Instruct them to fasten the pieces of fruit on their tree with the push-pins.

Point to the first tree and say to all the children, "Now you can see that this is an apple tree because it has apples on it." Point to the apples, but *ignore the oranges and cherries*. Point to the second tree and say, "This is an orange tree because it has oranges on it" – but *ignore the apples and cherries*. And, then, point to the third tree and say, "And this is a cherry tree because it has cherries on it," while *ignoring the apples and oranges*.

Look quite satisfied with yourself as you successfully identify the trees. However, the children will be quick to point out that there are different fruits on each tree.

Then say to the first child, "Then you get all the apples and put them on your tree"; to the second child, "You get all the oranges and put them on your tree"; and to the third child, "You get all the cherries and put them on your tree." This will cause a little confusion; but if you help them along, it will add to the humor of each child gathering the proper fruit while also delivering the message, "By their fruits you will know them."

When the children have completed this task – and it should be done fairly quickly – then point out that it is by the fruit on the tree that we finally know what kind of tree each one is. (This is especially important for the little ones who think that all fruit comes in plastic bags from the supermarket!)

Now put the three fruit trees aside (you have made your point), and introduce the fourth tree, the evergreen tree. Ask what kind of tree this is, and some of the children will be able to tell you. Then ask why it is called an evergreen, and some of them will know that, too. (As usual, if it should happen that no one has the answer, explain it to them.) Then say, "But this is also a "Catholic Tree! It's evergreen because we must be good Catholics *all year round*. How do you think people will know we are Catholic Trees?" Usually someone will say, "By the fruits on the tree." If not, simply prompt the answer by asking how they knew what kind of tree the others were.

Here is where you bring forth the eight or nine yellow circles (with push-pins) and say, "These are the fruits of a good Catholic." As you mention each one, stating briefly what each means, you pin it on the evergreen tree. When you have completed this part, hold up the Catholic Tree, and encourage each of them to try to be a good Catholic Tree that day. If they try to do the good things on the tree, people will know that they are Catholics by all the good fruit they have on their tree.

7

Let's Celebrate Mass with Flash Cards

(Mass, Multipurpose Teaching Device)

Since the approach is somewhat different, this homily should be given at the *beginning* of the Mass, for reasons that will quickly become obvious. It does constitute a homily, since it is on a liturgical subject (they don't *all* have to be on the Scriptures); and for equally obvious reasons, there need not be a homily at the usual time (unless, of course, you want to really tie up the parking lot between Masses).

One of the great challenges for teachers of the faith to children (or to adults, for that matter) is to make the Mass understandable. How many times have we heard them ask, "What's happening now?" or "Why is the priest doing that?" or a similar question revealing little understanding of what the Mass is all about. Naturally, with little children we can't get into a theological presentation on the sacrificial nature of the Mass or the Mass as a sacred meal. However, there is a way that helps the children get started on a basic understanding of why we celebrate and why we use the things we use at Mass.

The key word is CELEBRATE. Children know about celebrations. They celebrate birthdays and special holidays. They celebrate beginnings and endings of school (now there are even graduations from *pre*school!), so let's emphasize the celebrative aspect of the Mass as something to which they can relate; let's consider it a *party*! As we do so, we will employ flash cards to identify the things we use, and thus prepare for the Mass by involving the children in the preparation.

PROPS

You will need 19 cards made from poster board. They should be approximately 24" x 8" in size, and the printing should be large and all in uppercase. In that way, every child who knows the letters of the alphabet can at least come close to identifying the words by recognizing the letters.

The words to be printed on the cards will be given in **BOLD PRINT**, as we go through this exercise. Every card will have printing on both sides — in a few instances, with the same word(s) on both sides. The words on the back of the card should be printed upside down (in relation to the words on the front) so that reversing the card to show both sides means turning (flipping) the card over from top to bottom, rather than from end to end. This is especially helpful when you ask children to turn a card over. It is easier for them to hold it at the ends and flip it over than to turn it end for end. The flash cards should be in order and placed on a small table in the sanctuary, or simply brought forward by the celebrant. Less preferable is to have them on the altar, because we want to start with the altar bare of everything, including the altar cloth. The homilist should be in his street clothes, with each of the items to be identified somewhere within reach. They are placed on the altar as they are named.

HOMILY

Before the gathering song and Sign of the Cross, begin by talking about celebrations, asking the children to tell what they do to celebrate birthdays and holidays. Asking children questions can be tricky at times, as you never quite know how they are going to understand the question. Some hilarious answers can be given. And if you are alert and relaxed with the kids, you can turn them to your own advantage; or just laugh along with the adults who are listening, thus revealing your own humanity — something many of our churchgoers don't often experience!

It shouldn't take long to have them tell you they celebrate with a party — and you should pick up on that right away. Why? Because *the Mass is a party*. Yes, we use it to celebrate God's goodness to us, especially in the way Jesus shows His love for us. So you'll ask the children to try to think of all the things we use and do at a party. The technique for discovering these things will be 19 questions, with 19 flash cards:

1. "What is the most important piece of furniture in the room where the party is to be held? The answer is a **TABLE**." Show the card. "The table we use at Mass is, of course, the **ALTAR**." The word ALTAR should be on the reverse of the side printed "TABLE" so that

the children learn a new word for the special table used at our "church party." Reverse the card to show the word ALTAR. Then ask for one of the children to hold the card up for all to see. This gets them involved in a very simple but, for them, special way.

2. "What do we put on the table? A **TABLECLOTH**. What do we call the special cloth that goes on our altar/table?" Again, on the reverse side of the card, the answer "**ALTAR CLOTH**" is printed. Give this card to another child to hold. You will do this with all 19 cards. If you are working with the really little ones (up to the second grade), have them stand in the order in which the cards are introduced. If you are working with grade school children up to the sixth grade, *don't* have the children stand in order. Mix them up around the sanctuary so that, at the end of the homily, as you review the various cards, at least the older children will be challenged to remember each item in order. (By the way, I have used this with children up to the sixth grade; if you do this presentation with enthusiasm, they will vie for a chance to hold the cards!)

3. "How do we dress up our table? With **FLOWERS**." Show the card, give it to a child, and then either point to the flowers in the sanctuary or (a less preferable place) a small vase of flowers on the corner of the altar (*not in the middle*, where it will block the view of some of the items introduced later). If you want to introduce a note of humor here, before you hand the card to the child, say, "And what do we call the flowers used to decorate the altar?" Turn the card over and show that the other side also reads, "**FLOWERS**." This will show a contrast with the previous two cards and also that we don't have special names for everything.

4. "What else do we place on the table to make it look fancy? **CANDLES**." Again, use the same word on both sides of the card. (From here on, unless there is a special note I wish to add, I will give just the question and the answer flash card, leaving it to you to provide the commentary on each item.)

5. "What else can we put on the table? **PLACE MAT/CORPORAL**."

6. "Is there some other piece of cloth (or paper) for the person sitting at the place mat to wipe things with? **NAPKIN/ PURIFICATOR**."

7. "Do we need dishes? Yes! So we use a **PLATE/PATEN** for the food and . . .
8. . . . a **CUP/CHALICE** for the drink."
9. "How about the food? Don't we have special **FOOD** at a party? Yes! And at this party, the Mass, we have **BREAD**.
10. "And what about **DRINK**? There is **WINE**."
11. "When he celebrates the party that is the Mass, the priest has to have clean hands (and so do *you*!), and he also has to clean the cup at the end, so we use **WATER**."
12. "What do we do at a party?" (Here's where you have to "guide" the answers in the direction you want to go.) "We tell **STORIES**. The stories we tell at Mass are from a special book, the **BIBLE**. And the ones we choose for Mass are in a special collection of stories [the Lectionary]."
13. "We also play games at parties, and we need **GAME RULES**. While we don't play games at Mass, we do have rules for what we are to say and do at Mass, and these are in a special **PRAYER BOOK** [the Sacramentary]." You might want to display the pages of the Sacramentary, showing how the words are in black but the directions for the priest are in red.
14. "What else do we do at parties? We **SING**! So we have special **MASS SONGBOOKS** for our party, the Mass." (You might want to hold up a songbook from the pew.)
15. "What else do we do at parties? We **DANCE**! Yes, at Mass we do a kind of dance when we move about very slowly four different times. We call these times **PROCESSIONS**. They are the Entrance Procession, the Presentation of the Gifts Procession, the Communion Procession, and the Closing Procession."
16. "If we are the host or hostess at the party, we usually get dressed up in special **PARTY CLOTHES**. Since the priest is the person who is leading us at the Mass, he also wears special clothes called **VESTMENTS**." *As you show the three vestments,* **put them on.** *When you are finished, you will be all set to celebrate the Mass.*
17. "There is a long white robe to make the priest look nice and clean: the **ALB**. This reminds us of the white robe each one of us wore when we were baptized and became Catholics."

18. "There is a special piece around his neck to show that he is acting as a priest: the **STOLE**." (For older children, I compare it to a judge's robes, which he wears only when he is officially acting as a judge. Otherwise, he wears a suit.)
19. "There is a special robe to show that this is a very important party and, by its color, to show what time of year it is: the **CHASUBLE**. Its name means 'little house,' because it covers us up like a little house!"

You can conclude by proclaiming, "Now that we have all the things we need for a special party, let's celebrate!"

I have used the above homily for children from kindergarten through the fifth or sixth grade. Naturally, I don't use all 19 items for the little ones, but try to determine beforehand just how much they can handle, according to the circumstances, and perhaps after a conference with their teacher. I have found that, whatever number of items you use, this presentation holds their attention throughout because, although new things are being introduced all the time, none is very taxing on their imagination, and you are relating the new things to party items they're already familiar with. Moreover, the older children take great pride in being able to identify all the parts when I review them just before the Mass actually begins.

Depending on the amount of time one has, each celebrant will determine how much each or some of the items can be embellished. Simple as it may be (i.e., just a series of flash cards combined with the objects we use at Mass), I have found this to be one of the strongest teaching devices I have ever used. It also serves our purpose well — to give the children a greater familiarity with all the things we use at Mass, as well as a new framework in which to view the Mass: The Mass is a party!

*(A word of advice: This presentation serves as a wonderful class for those preparing for First Holy Communion. However, if you are going to use it as a Sunday homily, **be sure to announce it the week before, both at the beginning of Mass and in the parish bulletin**. Otherwise, those who arrive after you begin will think you have forgotten how to say Mass!)*

8

Martha and Mary

(Mass, Service, Hospitality)

This Gospel story (see Lk 10:38-42; 16th Sunday of the Year, Cycle C) was quite a challenge to present to children. What I finally developed was used at Camp Marist for Boys in New Hampshire, where I spend my summer vacations and where I have developed a number of the homilies in this book. So what follows is best used for children from second grade and up.

However, it contains a device that can be used to make presentations to all age groups. It replaces the need for a blackboard or newsprint, has everything prepared (so there is no time taken to write anything during the homily), and is far more colorful than a blackboard (no pun intended). Since it involves only printing words, all that you need are a variety of color marking pens and the time to lightly pencil in the letters — to make sure they all fit! (The real time, of course, is spent in developing an economy of words to convey your message. That's where the prayer time comes in.)

When confronted with making this Gospel applicable to children, this was the result. The story line was to be in words, not pictures, so I endeavored to present the words in a different and attractive way.

PROPS

I used a series of cards cut from poster boards, which were of three different colors. As you probably know, poster board comes in a standard size of 28" x 22". For this presentation, the pieces were all the same width (the standard 28" width of poster board), and I cut either two or three pieces from each sheet so they were either 7" or 11" in height. Whether they were 7" or 11" depended on whether I wanted to print one or two lines of text on each.

The pieces (a total of eight) were fastened to one another by strips of decorative plastic tape applied to the underside of the pieces so that the tape would not show. (I find the plastic tape stronger and more durable for this than Scotch tape.) This allowed me to fold the pieces accordion-style and place them on a table in front of the altar. The top piece was fastened to a piece of wood, 2 1/2" x 1" x 29". To each end of this piece, I screwed an eye from a hook-and-eye combination (available from your custodian or a hardware store). The two hook parts were attached at the end of two poles, 1 1/2" x 1" x 5'.

After I revealed the first three or four cards (or panels) myself, I employed two altar servers to come forward, hook the poles to the 29" crosspiece, and then they gradually lifted the whole thing, unfolding it piece by piece as I cued them. This was not only a colorful and novel way to present the ideas, but the method held the attention of everyone in the chapel as they waited to see what would be on the next panel. (See illustration. Note that only the first seven cards are shown.)

HOMILY

As an introduction, ask whether the children have ever had a party at their house. Then ask them what we call the person who gives the party; the answer is *host* or *hostess*. Then ask what the basic ingredients of a party are: the answer is *conversation* and *food*. At this time, display Card 1, on which are written the words "**HOST and HOSTESS**" and "**CONVERSATION and FOOD**."

Ask who the host or hostesses were in the Gospel story. The answer is (Card 2) "**Mary and Martha**" and "**The Guest Is Jesus**."

Then remark that very soon (Card 3) "**Jesus Is the Host**" because He led the conversation (with Mary) and shared the food (with Martha). He does the same with us. He provides (Card 4) the "**Conversation — The Bible**" and the "**Food — Holy Communion**." Here explain how the Mass is the "party" we are invited to and how the Liturgy of the Word is a conversation with God: in the First Reading, God speaks to us; in the Responsorial Psalm, we speak to God. The conversation goes on with the Second Reading (God) and the Verse before the Gospel (us), then the Gospel and Homily (God) and the Creed and General Intercessions (us). Then the bread and wine are changed into Jesus, and we receive the Food.

The next panel tells us that at Mass (Card 5) "**We Are the Guest**." Then (Card 6) "**We Listen to Jesus**" (conversation) and "**We Receive Jesus**" (food). But then (Card 7) "**We Are the Host!**" This is true because if we truly listen to what Jesus says and act like people who have received Him, then (Card 8) "**We Do What Jesus Tells Us**" and "**He Does It With Us**" because He is within us, encouraging us and showing us the way. (With the whole presentation held up in front of them, it is easy to review the entire lesson.)

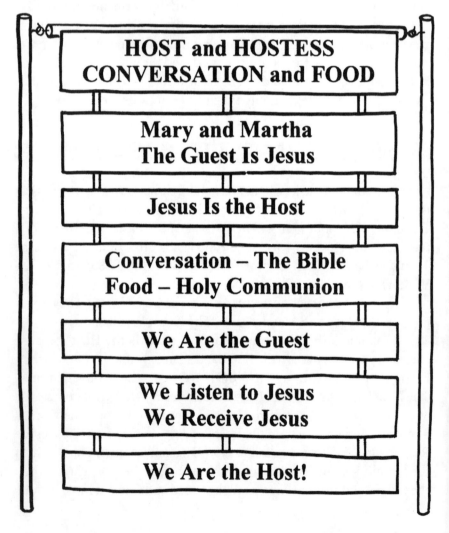

HOST and HOSTESS
CONVERSATION and FOOD

Mary and Martha
The Guest Is Jesus

Jesus Is the Host

Conversation – The Bible
Food – Holy Communion

We Are the Guest

We Listen to Jesus
We Receive Jesus

We Are the Host!

You may judge that you want to stop the development of this presentation after Cards 5 or 6, according to the age of your audience and/or their ability to grasp any more than that. Right now that decision is secondary. The principal point of my offering this method of presentation is twofold: (1) If you have a Gospel reading that is difficult to illustrate for children in anything other than words, then try to make the words as visually attractive and engaging as you can; and (2) the method of gradually unfolding the cards holds the children's attention right to the end. It also allows you to have the whole series of cards displayed with the help of only two other people (the altar servers), and the entire presentation is visible to the children at the end.

As noted above, this technique could be used for any series of phrases or short sentences you wish to use to develop a homily.

SECTION II

SEASONS

9

The Jesse Tree

(Advent, Christmas)

We are all aware of the steady influence of commercialism on our society in general, and on our children in particular, especially at Christmas. The total emphasis seems to be on Santa and the gifts he will bring. We try our best to distract them and direct their focus on the fact that "Jesus is the reason for the season," but it is often easier said than done. One of the best ways I know of to bring the proper central figures into focus and to do it in a story (something no one can resist) is to tell and illustrate the story of the Jesse Tree. The preparation may take some time, but it is well worth the effort. And once all of the ingredients are together, it can become an annual presentation, not just a one-time thing.

PROPS

Use a large piece of foam core (40" x 60"), on which you draw the outline of an evergreen tree. Next you need to draw on art board or poster board the various symbols indicated on the list at the end of this chapter and which are cued throughout the homily. (Otherwise have someone else draw them for you or copy, enlarge, and color the drawings provided in this chapter, or use them as templates.) These should be large enough to be seen at a distance. Details in the drawings are not as important as clarity and color.

Finally, you need as many pushpins as you have symbols. My suggestion is to begin placing the apple on the lower-left corner of the tree, then the next few symbols across the bottom, then zigzag up the tree, row by row, until you place the Infant Jesus (or star) at the top. The only exception would be the name **JESSE**, which should be the trunk of the tree.

You could also simply tell the story or read it as if from a book, while an assistant places the symbols on the tree. The assistant could even be dressed as an angel or a prophet.

At the end of this chapter, you will find examples of the drawings we used for the symbols. Notice their simplicity; they are done in coloring-book style. You can trace them and then color them in – and please make the colors bright! Note also that these examples are reductions of the actual symbols, so you can resize them as needed.

HOMILY

Here's the story you can tell:

"The Jesse Tree tells the story of God's saving love for all humankind, even after the first humans sinned against Him. He promised to send a Savior, who would redeem (that is, buy back) the human race from their sinful ways and make it possible for us to share in the eternal life of God in heaven. This was His original plan.

"When God created Adam and Eve, He placed them in the very beautiful and peaceful Garden of Eden (or Garden of Paradise). He gave them control over the whole garden, but placed a tree in the center of it that bore a fruit they were forbidden to eat. It was called the Tree of the Knowledge of Good and Evil.

"The Devil came in the form of a snake and tempted them to eat it, saying that if they did, they would be like God because they would know good from evil. Eve first ate the fruit (**APPLE**) and then gave it to Adam. They both disobeyed God by eating the fruit, and they truly came to know good from evil because, by sinning, they introduced evil into the world. God banished them from the garden, sentencing them to live 'by the sweat of their brow' and saying they would know suffering, pain, and death. However, He also promised to send a Savior to win back for them the right to live with God, provided they did His will.

"The people multiplied and began spreading throughout the world, and many of them sinned. God called Noah and told him to build a large boat (**ARK**), on which he was to make room for all his family, and two animals of every species on earth. There followed a flood that lasted 40 days and 40 nights. At the end of the rains, Noah sent out a **DOVE** to find dry ground, but it returned because the waters had not yet receded. Again he sent out the dove, and this time it returned with an olive branch in its beak, indicating that the waters had receded, and that it was safe to reestablish homes on the earth. (*Suggestion: Use a dove with an olive branch.*)

"God also said He would place a **RAINBOW** in the sky as a sign of the first covenant He made with humans. (A covenant is an agreement that would always bind the one who initiated it, even if the other person broke it.)

"God's next covenant with humans was through an old man who was wealthy and retired. God called him to take his family and flocks and move to a new and strange land. The man's name was **ABRAM**. Although the man had never known this God before, he obeyed, and God promised to make him the father of many nations, with descendants as numerous as the stars in the sky and the sands on the seashore. So God changed the man's name to **ABRAHAM**, which means 'father of many nations.'

"Though the man and his wife were very old, God promised them a son who would give them the first of these descendants. They did have a child, whom they named Isaac. In time, God told Abraham to take his young son Isaac up to the mountain and sacrifice him. Even though Abraham knew that would be the end of his chance to have grandchildren, he obeyed. Abraham told Isaac to get a **BUNDLE OF STICKS**, to put them on his back, and to travel up the mountain to the altar of sacrifice there. (This was a foreshadowing of God the Father asking His Son, Jesus, to carry the cross up the mount, or hill, of Calvary, to die there for all humankind.)

"Just as Abraham was about to slay his son, the angel of God appeared and told him not to do it. Abraham had proven his great faith in God and would be rewarded by becoming the father of God's people, just as God had originally promised.

"Isaac then had a son named Jacob, who, in turn, had 12 sons. These sons would be the heads of the 12 tribes that would make up the Chosen People. God changed Jacob's name to **ISRAEL**, thus giving the name used for the Chosen People. (This is why Jesus chose 12 apostles to be the leaders of the 'Chosen People' of the New Testament, the Church.)

"Jacob's favorite son was Joseph, to whom he gave a **COLORFUL COAT**. His brothers were jealous of him, and when they got the chance, they sold him as a slave to traders from Egypt. Joseph was taken there and was made a servant in the court of Pharaoh, the leader of Egypt. He was seen to be very talented and so was made the chief minister of

Egypt. Joseph also predicted that there would be a seven-year famine, so he ordered huge storehouses to be built to hold lots of wheat for use during the famine. When the famine came, the only country ready for it was Egypt.

"Jacob (Israel) sent some of his sons to Egypt to get some of the grain. Joseph recognized them (though they did not recognize him) and told them to go back to their homeland and return to him with their father and all his family. When they did this and came to Egypt, Joseph revealed his identity, and they were all reunited. This is how the Israelites, who were also called Hebrews, came to be in Egypt.

"Under the next Pharaoh, the Israelites were placed into slavery and forced to make the bricks with which the pyramids and other great buildings were constructed. God sent Moses to lead the people out of Egypt. God sent nine plagues as signs of His power to convince Pharaoh to let His people go free, but each time Pharaoh stubbornly refused.

"God then sent the tenth plague, and the angel of death slew the first-born of every family and flock in Egypt. Before this, God told the Israelites to prepare to flee with whatever they could carry, taking only unleavened bread (that is, bread without yeast) for food. They were also told to kill a **LAMB**, place some of its blood on the doorposts of their homes, roast the lamb, and eat it, and then be ready to escape. This was the Passover: the angel of death 'passed over' the Hebrews' homes (the ones with the lamb's blood on the doorposts) and did not kill any of them. Indeed, when Pharaoh saw the destruction that God had caused, he ordered the Israelites to leave. Moses led the people out of Egypt in what is now known as the Exodus.

"When Pharaoh realized he had made a mistake by letting all this slave labor go free, he sent his army after them. When the Israelites came to the Red Sea, with the Egyptian army in pursuit, they thought they would be killed there. However, God told Moses to wave his **STAFF** over the sea, and the waters parted, allowing the people to cross to the other side. When the Egyptian army pursued them, Moses waved the staff again and the waters flowed back, drowning the Egyptian soldiers. These two events, the Passover and the Exodus, became the high points in the history of God's relationship with the Hebrews, the people of Israel.

"As Moses led the people across the desert toward the Promised Land, he was called to the top of Mount Sinai, where God presented him with the **TEN COMMANDMENTS**. These were to be the new sign of the covenant between God and His people. Once they were in the desert, God provided the Israelites with food (manna and pheasants) and water. The water was obtained when God told Moses to strike a rock with his staff, and then water came from the rock. Because Moses struck the rock twice instead of only once (as though he really didn't think one strike would be enough), God said Moses would be punished by not being allowed to lead the people into the Promised Land.

"When Moses died in the desert, Joshua was appointed to lead the people. As Joshua led the Israelites into the Promised Land, he had to conquer the city of Jericho. It was a well-fortified city with a strong army. However, God told Joshua to have his army march around the city once each day, for six days. On the seventh day, they were to march around it seven times, and then the priests were to blow their horns (**TRUMPET**). When they did so, the walls tumbled down, and the Israelites captured the city.

"After the Hebrews settled in the Promised Land of Israel, they were often disobedient toward God, so God sent men to speak to them and bring them back to live His way. These men were called prophets, and the greatest of these was Isaiah (**SCROLL**). They also made predictions about the coming of the Savior, or Messiah ('the Chosen One').

The Hebrews wanted a king to rule over them, so God selected the son of **JESSE**. His name was David, whose hometown was Bethlehem. He became the greatest king (**CROWN**) in the history of the Israelite nation. It was also foretold that the Messiah would come from the house and family of David — that is, he would be a descendant of David.

" 'In the fullness of time,' an **ANGEL** announced to Mary (**LILY**) that she would be the mother of the Savior. She was engaged to Joseph, who was the town carpenter (**HAMMER and SAW**), and both of them were descendants of David.

"Her cousin Elizabeth was also going to have a child, John the Baptist, who would tell people that Jesus was coming. He baptized them to help them get ready to have their sins forgiven by Jesus (**WATER PITCHER**).

"Mary conceived, and just before she was to give birth, she and Joseph were ordered to go to **BETHLEHEM**, the city of David, to register for a census. It was there that the **INFANT JESUS** was born in a stable. While Jesus came as the Messiah and Savior to fulfill the promise God made at the beginning of the story, what is most unexpected about Him is that He is not only a man born of the Virgin Mary, but He is also the Son of God, thus making the Savior of the world the God-man. Only a God who loves us with an infinite and unconditional love would give so wonderful a gift as the gift of himself!"

(Note: If you wish, you can add to this narrative the story of the Three Wise Men, making symbols of **THREE CROWNS** *or the three gifts of* **GOLD, FRANKINCENSE, and MYRRH**. *You can also add the symbol of the* **STAR** *that appeared at the time of Jesus' birth. Other signs might suggest themselves as you go back over the entire story. The selection is up to the story-teller!)*

The Symbols and Their Meanings

APPLE
Symbol of Adam and Eve's original sin.

ARK
Symbol of God's mercy toward those who were faithful.

DOVE
Returned to the ark with an olive branch.

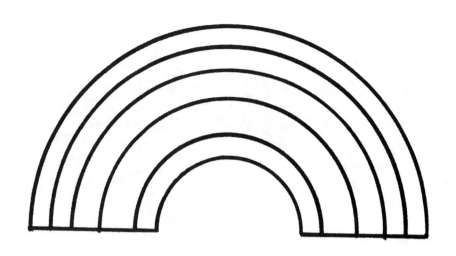

RAINBOW
Symbol of God's first covenant with His people.

ABRAM/ABRAHAM
Became "father of many nations."

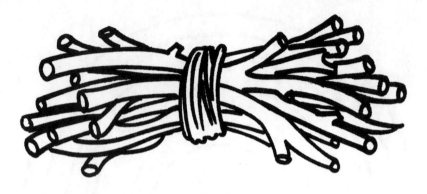

BUNDLE OF STICKS
Carried by Isaac up the mountain where he was to be sacrificed.

ISRAEL
Isaac's son Jacob, whose name became Israel;
also the name for God's Chosen People.

COLORFUL COAT
Owned by Joseph, whose brothers sold him into slavery in Egypt.

LAMB
Part of the Passover meal, its blood was sprinkled on the
Israelites' doorposts.

STAFF
Used by Moses to part the Red Sea and to strike the rock for water.

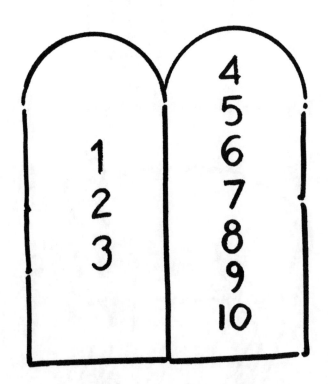

TEN COMMANDMENTS
God's laws given to Moses on Mount Sinai.

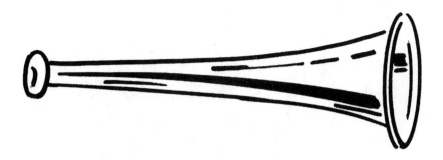

TRUMPET
Used by Joshua and the Israelites to bring down the walls of Jericho.

SCROLL
Symbol of Isaiah, greatest prophet who foretold
the coming of the Messiah.

CROWN
Symbol of David, greatest king of Israel; also, when three crowns, symbol of the Three Wise Men (or Three Kings).

JESSE
Father of King David (*attach this art to the bottom of the tree as its trunk*).

ANGEL
Announced to Mary that she would
be the mother of the Savior.

LILY
Symbol of Mary and her purity and virginity.

HAMMER and SAW
Symbol of Joseph the Carpenter.

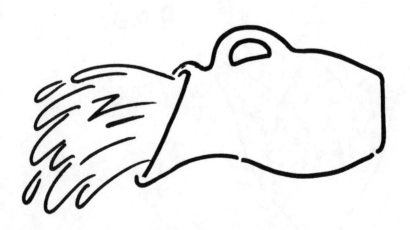

WATER PITCHER
Symbol of John the Baptist.

BETHLEHEM
City of David, Jesus' birthplace.

INFANT JESUS
Symbol of the God-man born in Bethlehem.

GOLD, FRANKINCENSE, and MYRRH
Gifts of the Three Wise Men.

STAR
Sign in the sky that appeared at the time of Jesus' birth.

10

A Christmas Homily in Pictures

(Signs and Symbols of Christmas)

Every Christmas Eve in our parish, we have a very special Family Mass, which, of course, calls for a special homily. There are a number of Christmas homilies in this book, so if you add this one, you will have enough to rotate from Christmas to Christmas for several years. I don't flatter myself thinking the children will remember what I did a few years ago. Besides, if the homily "works," then it deserves to be repeated. Moreover, there is a whole new group of children in place each Christmas that wasn't there years ago. So here is another Christmas homily for the Family Mass.

This particular Christmas homily accomplishes two goals. It defines 18 objects or symbols used at Christmas, thus educating the children (and those adults present) as to how these came to be used. Secondly, as you remove each of the symbols from the boards, you reveal letters, which form words that deliver a most important message about Christmas and why we celebrate it. So, there are two parts to the homily. In the first, you identify and explain the 18 Christmas symbols or objects displayed. Then, in the second, you remove them to reveal the message.

PROPS

You will need two large pieces of white foam core, 40" x 32".
On the first board print:

**THE BEST
REASON FOR
CELEBRATING
CHRISTMAS**

On the second board print:

**IT IS THE
BIRTHDAY
OF THE LORD
JESUS**

First Foam Core Board: Set a top and bottom margin of 3 1/2".
Using a pencil, draw the following lines:

THE BEST – Left and right margins should be 6". The letters should be in boxes 4" high and 3 1/2" wide, with the *letters* only 3" wide. Space between the words should be 3".

REASON FOR – Left and right margins should be 2". The letters should be as above, with a 3 1/2" space between words.

CELEBRATING – Left and right margins should be 1". The letters should be as above.

CHRISTMAS – Left and right margins should be 3 1/2". The letters should be as above.

Second Foam Core Board: Set the top margin at 3 1/2", and the bottom one at 2". Using a pencil, draw the following lines:

IT IS THE – Left and right margins should be 4 1/2". The letters should be in boxes 4" high and 3 1/2" wide, with the letters 3" wide. Space between the words should be 3".

BIRTHDAY – Left and right margins should be 6". The letters should be as above.

OF THE LORD – Left and right margins should be 1". The letters should be as above, with 3 1/2" between the words.

JESUS – Left and right margins should be 5 1/2". The letters should be in boxes 5 1/2" high and 5" wide, with 1" between the letters.

For the sake of variety and to add emphasis to some of the words, I would suggest that on the first board the words THE, REASON, and FOR be written in black; BEST in red; CELEBRATING in blue; and CHRISTMAS in alternating red and green.

On the second board, write IT in black; IS in blue; THE in orange; BIRTHDAY in alternating red and green; OF in black; THE in blue; LORD in violet; and the letters of the word JESUS in red, blue, orange, green, and purple. Recall that the letters of JESUS are larger than all the rest.

Now that you have completed these two boards, the creation of the pictures that will cover them is next. You will need to draw and color 18 different pictures, each in different quantities. The number for each picture will depend on how often the letter it represents appears on the two boards. So, for example, there is one picture of the Bible because the letter "M" appears only once; there are five pictures of the symbol for Mary because the letter "I" appears five times; there are six pictures of an angel because the letter "R" appears six times, and so on.

With that scheme in mind, here are the pictures, the quantity for each, and the letter they are to cover: BIBLE - 1 - **M**; MARY - 5 - **I**; JOSEPH - 1 - **G**; ANGEL - 6 - **R**; STABLE - 4 - **O**; INFANT JESUS - 5 - **S**; SHEPHERD'S STAFF - 2 - **D**; STAR - 2 - **C**; CROWN - 2 - **F**; GOLD, FRANKINCENSE, and MYRRH - 2 - **L**; TREE - 4 - **A**; CANDLE - 3 - **B**; DECORATION - 2 - **N**; CANDY CANE - 1 - **Y**; SANTA - 5 - **H**; WREATH - 8 - **T**; HOLLY - 7 - **E**. The final picture is one of BETHLEHEM, a silhouette of the city, which should *completely cover* the name JESUS.

Note that the pictures in this chapter are in black and white, but you should duplicate their outline and then color them with bright colors. Some of these illustrations are found in Chapter 9: Angel, Infant Jesus, Star, Crown, Bethlehem; and Gold, Frankincense, and Myrrh.

One of each picture should be drawn in color on a piece of white paper, 3 1/2" x 4". (Of course, only one Bethlehem picture is needed, on a larger piece of paper, 29" x 5 1/2".) Arrange these on pages to bring to a quick-print store to be copied. Then cut them out, and mount each picture on a piece of poster board. Now using one pushpin per picture, fasten each of the pictures over the letter it represents — as indicated above — until all letters are covered.

HOMILY

Have the two boards either hidden from view until you use them or have them in the sanctuary, but with the display side turned away from the assembly. Then when you are ready to use them, have two of the altar servers bring them forward and hold them up for all to see. The appearance of so many signs and symbols will instantly draw the attention of those present and lead to your going through them and explaining each one in order. Here are a few sample explanations:

- The **wreath** is round for God's endless love, is green as a sign of hope, and has a red bow as a sign of love.
- The **holly** is green for hope, has sharp points to remind us of Jesus' suffering, and has red berries to recall the blood that He shed.
- The **candle** is a sign of Jesus as the Light of the World.
- The **candy cane** is a symbol of the Good Shepherd or of the shepherds at the stable. Reverse it and it is the letter "J" for Jesus: the white stands for His purity, and the red for His love.

The rest are self-explanatory.

After reviewing the signs and symbols, begin to remove the pictures in the order they appear on the boards: all the wreaths (T), then the Santas (H), and so on, thereby displaying all of each letter. Both children and parents will be intrigued to see the words on the boards slowly form until the entire message is displayed, the Bethlehem picture being last. When all the letters are uncovered, simply stress the message.

If it is the custom to have a Christmas pageant or tableau, set the scene for the members of the pageant to come forward and take their places. This can be done as you review the message on the two boards in a soft voice, creating an atmosphere of quiet. Then follow with a children's Christmas song (sung by the children's choir, if you have one), which should calm the kids down. Then send everyone back to their places, asking that they go in silence. If you ask in a nice paternal tone, they will!

BIBLE

SHEPHERD'S STAFF

TREE

MARY

JOSEPH

CANDY
CANE

DECORATION

HOLLY

CANDLE

STABLE

SANTA

WREATH

11

A Christmas Jigsaw Puzzle

(Nativity)

The Christmas Eve Family Mass always draws a huge crowd (in many places they arrive more than an hour early!), and it calls for a special homily. This is one that takes some time to make up, but it works very well — and after all, it *is* Christmas!

Essentially, it calls for making a jigsaw puzzle from a picture of the Nativity. During the homily, the pieces of the puzzle are mounted on a board, gradually producing the Nativity scene while you give a commentary. It also provides a fine background for the traditional pageant or tableau that can follow.

PROPS

You will need two pieces of foam core board, 32" x 40", one to make the puzzle and one to serve as a display board. You will also need a color picture of the Nativity scene. In addition, you will need a blade that will easily cut foam core; about 40 Velcro dots; black, green, and red felt-tip markers; and either a Christmas gift box or gift bag. Finally, you will need an easel on which to display the board.

1. Begin with a picture of the Nativity. I used one from the cover of a Christmas coloring book, the same one I used in the homily "The Reason for the Season." Have the picture blown up at your local printer. Then cut it up into 15 to 19 pieces, making the cuts in jigsaw interlocking style. (See Diagram 1.) If the resulting picture is not large enough to be seen from the rear of the church when fully assembled, have the *individual* pieces blown up so that, when they are all assembled, the picture is visible from the rear of the church. (The printer will know how to do this so that all the pieces are in the proper proportion.) The final puzzle-picture I used ultimately mea-

sured 32" wide by 33" high. (This was due to the original dimensions of the picture.) The picture fit perfectly on a piece of foam core, 32" x 40" — and even left a 7" margin at the top where I printed the words "**A CHRISTMAS PUZZLE**." (The pieces could also be cut simply into different shapes but with straight sides. That would make Step 2 easier, but the whole picture would lose the traditional jigsaw-puzzle look. (See Diagram 2.) **One very important point:** In whatever way you cut the pieces, *be sure that there is one that contains the Infant Jesus in the manger.* That is the last piece to be put in place, which brings the story to its logical climax, so be sure there is such a piece.

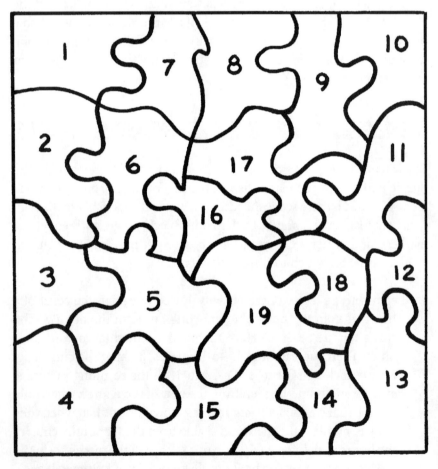

DIAGRAM 1

DIAGRAM 2

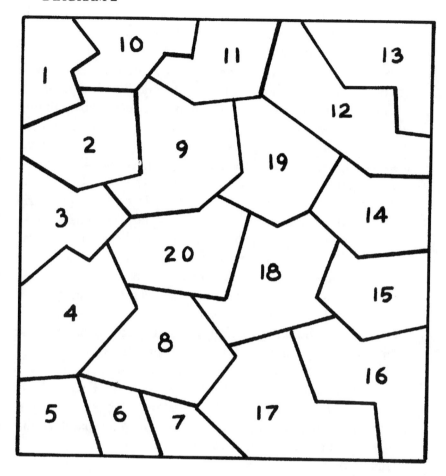

2. Once the pieces of the picture have been enlarged to the correct size, use your ever-faithful glue stick or spray mount to fasten each piece of the puzzle picture on a piece of foam core. Then use a sharp knife or a small saw to trim the foam core to the shape of the puzzle piece. I used the small saw on a Leatherman tool, and it worked just fine. (Perhaps a thin-blade hacksaw, or even a coping saw, would work.) An alternative (and preferred) method would be to lay out all the puzzle pieces in their proper places on a second piece of foam core (32" x 40") and use a pencil to trace the outline of each puzzle piece on the sheet of large foam core. The advantage here is that you will be cutting the pieces along adjacent lines and prob-

ably end up with the pieces fitting together more accurately. You may have to trim the pieces a bit — foam core does not cut smoothly when it is cut against the grain — but this can be done with an X-Acto knife or even sharp scissors.

3. When all the pieces are prepared, lay them out in their proper places on the large foam core board, and trace their outline onto the board. Decide what order you want to position them on the board during the homily, and use a magic marker or felt-tip pen to number each piece in that order. Use a pencil to write, in small numbers, the corresponding number on the large board, just large enough for you to see during the homily so that you will know what piece goes where.

4. Next, you need to attach two Velcro dots to the back of each puzzle piece. The dots should be the self-adhering kind. Remove the protective paper from one side of the first dot, and stick the dot near one end of the back of the puzzle piece. Then place the second dot on the piece some distance away from the first. Now with both pieces of Velcro still stuck together, remove the remaining protective piece from each dot. Then, following the outline of the pieces that you have drawn on the board, carefully press the piece against the large foam core board, being sure it goes in its proper location. You will find that the Velcro dots stick to the piece and to the board very well when you separate the piece from the board. Finally, remove all the pieces and place them into either a Christmas gift box or gift bag in the order in which you want to withdraw them for placement on the board. In this way, they are all in the same place and ready for attaching to the board.

5. The final step is to print across the top of the board (remember the 7" margin?) the words "**A CHRISTMAS PUZZLE**." To my surprise, an interesting side effect of the appearance of the board with this caption on top and all the black dots on it was that the children thought it was a connect-the-dots puzzle! When you show them it is a jigsaw puzzle instead, that provides an additional surprise.

6. I found it made things much easier if one of the older girls (a seventh- or an eighth-grader) was dressed in an angel costume and handed me the pieces; then I put them in place. If you really want to concentrate completely on telling the story accompanying the placement of the puzzle pieces, you could have the young lady — or even

a second "angel" – put the pieces in their proper places on the foam core board for you.

HOMILY

At the beginning of the Mass, the board on the easel should be placed off to the side of the sanctuary. When you are ready to begin the homily, bring the easel and board to the front of the altar. The pieces of the puzzle are in either a box or bag.

The actual text of the homily is self-evident. Begin to speak about the toys children get for Christmas and how one of the all-time favorites is a puzzle. Call attention to the board on the easel, and ask the kids what kind of puzzle they think this is. Most will say it is a connect-the-dots puzzle. That's when you surprise them by telling them it is a jigsaw puzzle.

Now introduce your Christmas angel, who brings out the Christmas box or bag containing the puzzle pieces. From here on, the homily will depend on the picture you used for the puzzle and the order in which you deal with the various figures in the picture. As each piece is placed on the board, talk about it and, should there be only part of a figure in the piece, then have the children try to guess who the whole person will be. Little devices such as this hold their interest and keep them wondering where you are going with the homily.

Once you put the figure of the Infant Jesus in place, then the puzzle is completed, and it is time to quickly review the story. Focus on the Infant Jesus, and lead into the pageant or tableau, if you have one. Finally, leave the puzzle on the easel, and place it in the sanctuary, where it is visible but out of the way for the rest of the Mass. If you so choose, you could even have it carried out in the Recessional by one of the altar servers, preferably a tall one who can hold it above his/her head so it can be seen by all and continue to focus their attention on the purpose of coming to the celebration.

12

A Christmas 'Show and Tell'

(Christmas Decorations)

This is a homily that works for everyone! I even used it once at Midnight Mass and received a very positive response. It really is a kind of Christmas "show and tell," with the various decorations being the *show* part and the explanation of how they contribute to a better understanding of Christmas constituting the *tell* part. In a sense, then, the props and their explanation constitute the homily. You will see what I mean as I list them and indicate their contribution to the Christmas message.

PROPS

You will need a large, colorful Christmas box, or one covered with Christmas wrapping paper, which states immediately that the contents relate to the feast. It also focuses attention on the box and "What will he take out next?" This is much better than having all the items displayed on a table so they are seen as soon as someone comes close to the sanctuary, thus removing some of the suspense and joyful surprise that you want in a homily, especially during Christmastide.

Inside the box are as many different items connected with Christmas as you can find (be ready to provide the reason for their use). This may take a trip to Christmas shops or similar places, but the variety of items will add considerably to the impact of the homily as well as to its instructional value. It is surprising how many people use Christmas decorations and other seasonal items without any idea as to how they originated.

HOMILY

Point out that we celebrate Christmas with a wide variety of decorations and other items, many of which carry a message about the feast and the principal reason for celebrating Christmas: the birth of Jesus. Then bring out the decorated box and, one by one, withdraw each item and give the explanation as to why we use each of them at Christmastide. Here are some suggestions (you can add or subtract according to your desire):

1. **Christmas tree** (a small one, either real or artificial, but clearly evergreen. It need not be decorated). The evergreen tree is actually an ancient pagan symbol of the constancy of life. Its use goes back a long time before the birth of Jesus. As far as we know, the Germans of the 18th century were the first to use it as a Christmas symbol, since the evergreen stood for God and the eternal life He has, which He promises to give to those who are faithful. Germans brought the custom to America in the 19th century. The color green is also a sign of hope, especially the hope given by God, through the prophets, that the Son of God fulfilled by becoming man. It also symbolizes the hope that Jesus gives us if we follow Him faithfully.

2. **Wreath**. Its shape (a circle) tells us of the eternal life of God, which has no beginning or end. (That's why we don't have square Christmas wreaths!) Again, the evergreen wreath tells us the same message as does the tree. If there is a red bow on it, the red can stand for love, the love revealed by God in sending us His Son.

3. **Holly**. The holly is green (see above), the sharp prickle reminds us of the Passion of Jesus, and the red berries tell us that He came to shed His blood for us. You might want to quote the words from the carol "The Holly and the Ivy": "The holly bears a berry,/As red as any blood,/And Mary bore sweet Jesus Christ,/To do poor sinners good./ The holly bears a prickle,/As sharp as any thorn,/And Mary bore sweet Jesus Christ,/On Christmas Day in the morn." If the wreath is made of holly, then this explanation can be added to that of the wreath.

4. **Candle**. Light the candle, in a holder, and then state that it stands for Jesus, the Light of the World, who came to shatter the darkness of sin and to light our way so we can follow Him to the Father in heaven. If the candle is red, remark again about the color red standing for the love Jesus came to show as He leads us to the Father; if it's green, then it can be another sign of hope. The German people put candles on their Christmas trees to symbolize the new life Jesus, the Light of the World, came to bring.

5. **Candy cane**. This symbolizes the shepherd's crook, which reminds us that the poor, humble shepherds were the first ones to be told about the birth of the Savior. It also calls to mind that Jesus is the Good Shepherd, who guides us and watches over us as the shepherd does his sheep. If you turn the cane upside down, it forms the letter "J" for Jesus. The colors are also symbolic: white for His purity, and red is for His love. (Sometimes there is a green stripe that stands for the hope He came to give us all.)

6. **Star**. This should be large enough to be seen by all the children. It reminds us of the star that God sent to lead the Three Wise Men to the place where Jesus and Mary were. It also tells us of one of the names given to Jesus — Morning Star — because it marks the beginning of a new day. Jesus marks the beginning of a whole new way of life for all people who follow Him.

7. **Santa Claus**. Explain that Santa takes his name from St. Nicholas (from the Dutch *Sinterklaas*, which was altered from *Sint Nikolaas*). And just as St. Nicholas, the bishop of Myra, was famous for giving gifts to the poor, so Santa is famous for giving gifts to all children who are good. (*Note: **Be careful that you do not take away any of the mystique of Santa!** To do so will confuse the little ones, give undue stature to the "more mature," and perhaps more importantly, bring down upon you the wrath of the parents! When the children finally do discover that there is no Santa, let that news come from someone other than you.*)

8. **Beautifully wrapped present**. We give gifts to one another at Christmastide as a symbol of the greatest gift that has ever been given to the world: Jesus, the Son of God and our Savior.

9. **Crèche**. This should be large enough so it can be seen by all those present. It can be fashioned in such a way that all the pieces are attached to a base so that the whole thing can be shown at once. Or the individual figures could be lying down on your table when you begin; then you simply stand them up in their proper place when it is time to focus on the stable scene. Perhaps it would be easier just to have a large colored picture of the Nativity scene, or just the three main figures — Jesus, Mary, and Joseph — and show these.

10. **Christmas song and carol book**. Few things connect us with Christmas more than the music of the season. When we take the time to read the words, not just sing them, most of the carols speak with

greater theological insight more often than we realize. So find a colorful Christmas carol book, select two of the carols, and read the verses that tell most eloquently of the great mystery of God's love that we are celebrating. This will be especially meaningful for the adults who are present.

Here is another suggestion: Instead of the whole Nativity scene, you might just use a fairly large figure of the Infant Jesus. This could be produced from the beautifully wrapped present and shown as the greatest gift of all. In that case, of course, the beautifully wrapped present would be the last item shown.

Hold each of these items up high so that they can be clearly seen by all. Then arrange them in whatever manner allows them to be seen throughout the rest of the Mass or service without blocking the view of the altar. Perhaps you could place a table in front of, but lower than, the altar. (Be aware that you might then have to rearrange or even remove some of the flower decorations for the duration of that Mass.) By all means, make sure that at the conclusion, the Nativity scene or the figure of the Infant Jesus is front and center, displayed as the most important of all the items. Indeed, it is the one that gives all the others their meaning.

13

The Reason for the Season

(Nine Gifts of Christmas)

Since we have a very special celebration for the children on Christmas Eve in our parish, there is a need to keep coming up with something fairly new almost every year. That is quite a challenge, yet the more than 300 youngsters who crowd into that magical, mystical Christmas Eve Mass each year and who sit on the floor of the sanctuary during the homily would be sorely disappointed if there were not something special for them, along with the "required" Nativity-scene pageant. The following idea came to me while reading one of the magic publications to which I subscribe. The presentation requires no skill whatsoever. It is literally self-working, works very well, holds the children's attention throughout, and delivers a very important message.

PROPS

You will need nine pictures that deal with the things of Christmas. They can be already printed or you can develop them yourself, as I did, by finding a coloring book that contains the pictures you need. (Let me say right here that I know that Christmas may well be the busiest time of the year, so once again I encourage you to enlist the assistance of people in your parish. They will be very eager to help you and to be part of what they will consider a most important event.)

There are two reasons why I choose to use coloring books. First, the children are used to dealing with these, and when colored in, the pictures are always in solid colors and clearly outlined. The second reason is that all the pictures will then have a uniformity of style to them. (It's a good idea to buy two copies of each, just in case you mess up while coloring one!) While developing this homily, I first checked with my schoolteachers and CCD teachers to see if they had any pictures I could use. I did come across some beautiful pictures of the Nativity, but I felt that the variety of styles would detract from the point I was trying to make.

From the coloring books, choose nine pictures of things pertaining to Christmas, making sure that there is one of the Christ Child in the manger. (HE is the "reason for the season," in case you haven't figured that out from the title yet!) Remove those pictures from the books, and take them to your local quick-print store to have them copied. *Do this before you color them!*

I made the mistake of coloring one first, only to find out that the markers bleed through the page, rendering the other side of the page useless. Also, because of the kind of paper most coloring books are printed on, the black lines on the reverse side of a page show up in the picture you want copied. The printer can eliminate this problem for you.

Once you have clear copies made, use felt-tip markers to color in the pictures. Do this carefully, especially if you use washable markers. Be sure to allow time for the colors to dry; otherwise they will smudge and ruin the picture. If you don't like to color (can't stay within the black lines?), or simply don't have the time, then call on those very willing parishioners mentioned above.

What nine pictures did I use? (1) Santa; (2) a tree with decorations and gifts; (3) the angel speaking to Mary; (4) Mary and Joseph; (5) the angel speaking to the shepherds; (6) the shepherds going to Bethlehem; (7) the Three Wise Men looking at the star and a map; (8) the Wise Men presenting their gifts; and (9) the Nativity scene, with Jesus as the central figure. (You could also use a picture of a wreath, holly, a candle, and so on, but there can only be nine pictures.)

For the last one (Jesus in the manger), I used the cover of a coloring book that had a beautiful picture of the Nativity scene. The fact that it was different from the other eight only enhanced its special position among them.

When Pictures 1-8 were all colored in, I cut the pictures out to eliminate as much of the margin as possible. These were brought to the printer, who enlarged them to fit a page measuring 11" x 14".

Using plain white poster boards (buy these in packs of ten – they're much cheaper!), cut out nine pieces, 22" x 14", which you then should crease in the middle so they fold over to measure 11" x 14". On the inside right-hand side, paste one of the pictures. Now do the same with the other eight pictures.

(Note: Here again I suggest that you use **spray mount,** *the spray rubber cement. It's available in art-supply stores or good office-supply stores. It's clean to handle, spreads easily, and won't cause bubbles under the paper the way rubber cement in a bottle does. It also won't bleed through, and it allows you to lift and reset a picture if you don't get it down exactly even the first time. It's great stuff!)*

Finally, get nine different kinds of Christmas gift wrap, and paste a sheet on the outside of each folder. You now have nine folders, each of which has a distinct outward look and a different picture inside.

The only things remaining are: (1) two posters (the size is up to you) with "**The REASON for**" printed on one and "**the SEASON**" printed on the other; (2) a Christmas tree ball that is unbreakable; and (3) a large red stick-on bow, the kind you put on a gift. Finally, arrange the folders in such fashion that, when the children hold them and you count from left to right, the folder with the Nativity scene is the *third* from the left.

Place the "The REASON for" sign on the top of the pile and the "the SEASON" sign on the bottom. You are now ready to begin. *(Note: You might want to number all of the folders so that you are sure they are in the order in which you want to open them as you tell your story.)*

HOMILY

Select nine children to hold the folders, and have them stand in a straight line across the sanctuary. Ask two altar servers to assist, posting one at each end of the line of nine children. Give the "The REASON for" sign to one of the servers, and have him/her stand at the beginning of the line. Then give each of the children one of the folders, being sure that the *third folder from the left* has the picture of the Nativity. Finally, "the SEASON" sign is given to the other server, who stands at the end of the line.

Now turn to the children in the assembly, and ask them what season they have just completed. The answer, of course, is Advent. Then ask what season they are beginning, the answer being Christmas. (Don't be surprised if one of the children says, "Winter!" Congratulate him/her on knowing this, and ask the question again. You won't have to ask it more than twice!) Say how very special this season is and how they are about to discover why it is so special.

Next take the unbreakable Christmas tree ball in hand, say that you will turn your back to the children and will toss it back over your head so that one of them can catch it. Instruct them that there is no prize for catching it, so they are not to jump up for it. Toss the ball and turn around to see who caught it. Now ask that child to turn his/her back to the group and toss it overhead as you did. Do this a third time. Now explain to them that you did this so that the person who ended up with the ball is a totally free choice; you did not pick the person.

Now point out to all present that there are nine folders; count aloud as you point to each so that all the children know that there are nine. Ask the child who has the unbreakable Christmas tree ball to call out a number from one to nine. State further that whatever number he/she selects will tell which of the folders has the answer to the question "What is the reason for the season?" To mark that folder, you will use the big red stick-on Christmas bow. (Have it ready at hand, and show it to the children as you say this. If you wish, you can let the child with the tree decoration hold it.)

Here is where the magic principle comes in:

- If the child says "ONE," ask the child if he/she can also spell that number. When the child says "Yes" (and if the child is little, he/she will love to show this off!), have the child do so. Starting at the first folder, spell aloud "O-N-E," pointing to each folder as you do so. This will bring you to the third (Nativity) folder, so stick the bow on that folder.
- If the child says "TWO," then proceed as you did with ONE.
- If the child says "THREE," then simply count "One, two, three" from the first folder, arriving at the Nativity folder and putting the bow on it.
- If the child says "FOUR," then ask him/her to spell the number, and this time starting at the sign at the beginning (the one reading, "The REASON for"), spell out "F-O-U-R." You will arrive at the Nativity scene.
- If the child says "FIVE," proceed as you did with FOUR.
- If the child says "SIX," proceed as you did with ONE and TWO.

- If the child says "SEVEN," begin counting one to seven from the *folder* at the end of the line (the folder before "the SEASON" sign). You will end at the Nativity folder.
- If the child says "EIGHT," begin counting one to eight from the *sign* at the end ("the SEASON").
- If the child says "NINE," proceed as you did for FOUR and FIVE.

In every case, you will always end at the Nativity folder. Please remember that you are only asking one child for one number. Therefore, if you actually do *count* the folders (and, if needed, a *sign*) for numbers three, seven, and eight, the assembly will presume that you would have counted the folders no matter what number the child selected. If the child's choice calls for you to use the *spelling* method (numbers one, two, four, five, six, or nine), the presumption will be that you would have done that no matter what number was chosen, giving the child a chance to show that he/she can spell. So no one will detect how you arrived at number three, the Nativity folder . . . unless there is a magician in the church! And he's not allowed to tell!

For all practical purposes, the work is done. Now go to each folder in whatever order you choose, open it to reveal the picture, and ask, "Is *this* the reason for the season?" (Don't be surprised if, at the picture of Santa, some of them answer, "Yes!") Then go on to explain how the picture shows something *about* Christmas, but that it is *not* "the reason for the season."

Finally, you will come to the folder with the Nativity scene in it, the one with the red bow on it. You open it, show it to everyone, and ask, "Is *this* the reason for the season?" The answer will be a resounding "Yes!" and your point will have been made. Don't stop there, however. Now, in summary fashion, review the other pictures, showing how they all play a part in our Christmas celebration (yes, even Santa and the tree), and then drive home the point for the last time that *Jesus is the reason for the season.*

Four helpful points:

1. Be sure to select children old enough to hold up the signs without getting tired. You might do this beforehand and simply invite those who were chosen to come to the sanctuary before inviting all the

other children to take their positions on the floor. That way the little ones don't feel rejected when they volunteer.

2. As you come to each folder, take it from the child, and hold it up high for everyone to see. Don't just play to the children up front. This homily is for everyone present, so they should all be able to see what you are holding up.

3. If you wish, try to obtain from one of the cut-rate religious-supply houses an inexpensive gift for each child present. These could be little cardboard pop-up Nativity scenes, a plastic decoration with a picture of the Nativity, or some such item. Have all these in three or four decorated bags or boxes, and ask the adults who are helping you to distribute the gifts as the children return to their seats. *Always be sure to buy more than you think you will need.* The one thing you clearly want to avoid is having a child not receive your gift.

4. If you have a Christmas pageant or tableau following the homily, have the characters come to the sanctuary and stand quietly behind the nine children and two servers who are holding the nine folders and two signs. Then, when the Nativity folder is selected and you complete your homily, collect the folders and signs, and have those holding them return to their seats. This reveals the pageant children, who can then take their positions for the pageant or tableau, and the choir can sing a special song while you stand next to the scene. (e.g., "Once in Royal David's City," "Away in a Manger," "Sleep, Holy Babe," "Silent Night"). Your quiet demeanor, along with the singing, will bring the reverent silence that you wish. Then (if all the children in the church had gathered up front for your homily) send all of the children back to their seats, with the gifts being distributed as they leave, and go on with the Mass.

14

Don't Ask How It Works — It Just Does!

(Christmas, Epiphany, Easter, and Other Times)

At a magic convention in July 1995, I saw a trick or magic principle demonstrated by a dealer who specializes in what is called "Gospel magic." Its use is common among fundamentalists but is something I have stayed away from. From time to time, I will use a trick to make a point (as I have in a couple of the items in this book). But the regular practitioners of Gospel magic usually take a trick and ask, "What Scripture passage can I find that will enable me to use this to get attention?" instead of asking, "Is there something I can use to help me demonstrate the lesson I want to teach?" — thus putting the emphasis on the passage and lesson rather than on the trick. I use magic in a homily, perhaps only twice a year, because I want the assembly to remember the *message*, not the magic.

However, this trick fascinated me because of the method used and the simplicity of it; it is mysterious and engaging, yet it takes no skill whatsoever. As a matter of fact, I honestly don't understand *why* it works; I only know that it does. If you are a mathematician, you may be able to explain it (I have been told it has something to do with a theory of probability), but that really is not important here. What is important is that anyone can do it, and with some thought, it can be used several times, each time delivering a different message.

PROPS

- An easel (or a child!) holding a sign that contains the message to be explained. The message contains a series of words printed large enough for all to see. The first word must have an odd number of letters. Each word (or combination of words) after the first has one less letter than the word(s) preceding. The final word of the message can be as long as needed, provided it has an odd number of letters. For example, the theme message I used for the feast of the Epiphany was (the words and the number of letters):

CELEBRATE (9)

EPIPHANY! (8)

JESUS IS (7)

SAVIOR (6)

OF ALL! (5)

LORD (4)

GOD (3)

OF (2)

NATIONS! (7)

To minimize the visible fact that the letters on each succeeding line are one less than those on the preceding line, I suggest that you print the first four or five lines on one poster board horizontally, and then print the remaining words on another poster board vertically. This also allows you to print in larger letters, giving better visibility for those at the rear of the church.

- Two sets of matching cards. One set has a different question on each card, and if possible, the front of each card is different in color. However, the backs of the cards should all have the same color. This can be achieved by computer printing the words for each card on different colored paper and then pasting each page to a piece of poster board, all the same color. The result is similar to a deck of cards, with a different face on each card but all having the same back design or color.

To provide a nice finished look to the cards, instead of using construction paper, go to a good stationery store and buy two each of as many pieces of stationery, of different colors or designs, as you will need. You will need one more card in each pile than you have letters on the first line of the theme statement. So, in our example, since there are nine letters in the first line, you will need two sets of *ten* cards each. The two sets of cards are, of course, identical.

To make them easy to handle and durable (easy to be kept clean), I suggest you take the cards to a print shop and have them laminated.

For the feast of the Epiphany, I used the following questions. (The answers are provided for quick reference.) Obviously, the answers should *not* be printed on the cards! Again, there are ten questions because there are nine letters in the first line of the theme message.

1. How many Wise Men were there? (We don't know. The number three comes from the number of gifts they brought.)
2. What were the names of the Wise Men? (We don't know. The names Caspar, Melchior, and Balthazar are fictional.)
3. What did the gift of gold signify? (Jesus is a King.)
4. What did the gift of frankincense signify? (Jesus is God.)
5. What did the gift of myrrh signify? (Jesus would die for us.)
6. What led the Wise Men to the Christ Child? (A star.)
7. Who said that Jesus would be born in Bethlehem? (The prophet Micah [see Mi 5:1].)
8. Where did the Wise Men find the Christ Child and Mary? (In their *house*, not in the stable [see Mt 2:11].)
9. Whom did the Wise Men ask for directions? (King Herod.)
10. Why did the Wise Men go home by a different route? (The angel warned them not to go back to King Herod.)

The two sets of cards are in identical order, and each set should be lying face down and fanned out. They are either on a tray or on the altar, so they can simply be picked up and the faces shown to the assembly.

- Because it was the feast of the Epiphany, I wanted to involve some of the children, so I went to the party store and bought two crowns. I then went to the fabric store and found material with stars printed all over it. I also bought a piece of gold roping and used these two items to fashion the typical desert headdress that you see in all the pictures of the Epiphany. When all the children had gathered at the altar for the homily, I selected three children of suitable age who could follow directions, and I gave each of them one of the head-pieces to wear. Then I asked two of them to handle the cards and the other to point to and read the lines on the theme message. (If you follow my suggestion about having the theme message printed on two cards, you will need a fourth child to assist, perhaps dressed as an angel.)

HOMILY

Actually, the homily consists of commenting on the theme message and then doing the trick, dealing with the questions on the cards in whatever order they are revealed. Therefore, there is one drawback with this method: that you have no way of knowing which cards will come up when. Now let's get to the working of this.

- Pick up and show that the two sets of cards are in identical order by holding them fan-like, one set in each hand, as you might with playing cards. Do not review the words on the cards, since that will spoil the contents of the presentation. Rather, call attention to the sequence of *colors* of the cards, and in this way show that the two piles match. Then turn them around so that it can be seen that the backs are identical.

- Close the two "fans," turn them facedown, and put one set on top of the other. State that now you will mix them by taking one card at a time off the top and putting it on the bottom until someone tells you to stop. Choose one of the children to say "Stop." Then move the cards, one at a time, from top to bottom.

- Stop when you are told to stop. Now invite two people to come up and stand next to you, one on either side. (If you have already chosen two "Wise Men," they will take these positions. The third "Wise Man" should stand next to the easel ready to read the theme message line by line.) Ask the person on your left to hold out both his hands, palms up. From the top of the facedown deck, deal off half the cards (in our example, *ten*) one at a time, one on top of the other, onto his hands, thus reversing the order. This leaves you with ten cards in the person's hands and ten in your hands. Simply fan these ten cards in your hands, their backs to the people, to show there are ten.

Now tell the person on your right to hold out his hands, palms up, and then deal the remaining ten cards onto his hands, but *deal from the bottom*. In that way, you will not reverse their order as you did with the first ten.

Throughout this procedure, the cards are kept facedown, so all are seen to have the same color backs. (At this point, if you were to turn faceup the pile the person on your left is holding, you would see that the cards are now in reverse order when compared to the ones on the other person's hand. However, *do not* turn any of the cards over at this time.)

• Ask one of the children to point to one of the "Wise Men" holding the card piles. When one is selected, point to the theme message (or have the third "Wise Man" do so), and tell them that you will spell the first line of the theme message (CELEBRATE) letter by letter. For each letter spelled out, the "Wise Man" holding that pile will move a card from the top of that pile to the bottom.

Moreover, before beginning, tell the child that he/she can switch to the other pile *at any time during the spelling,* and they can switch from one dealer to the other *as often as they wish* until the word is completely spelled out. They simply say, "Switch."

*(Note: It is very important to keep track of the counting process, making sure that **only one card** is moved from top to bottom for each letter spelled out. Sometimes, when the speller is switching piles, the person dealing the cards can lose track of the count. If that happens, the whole process is lost, so be alert!)*

The amazing thing (and the one that I don't understand!) is that, no matter how often they switch piles (or don't switch), when the spelling is finished, and the card on top of each pile is turned faceup, the cards will match! Once you see what question is on the two matching cards, you can answer the question and comment on it.

When you have finished commenting on the first question revealed on the two top cards, move on to the second line of the theme message, have that line read aloud, and then ask for another volunteer to pick a starting pile. Spell out the line on the theme message, and switch (or not switch) whenever desired. The results will always be that the top cards match.

Additional Suggestions

As further examples of the theme message, for Christmas you might use the theme message: CHRISTMAS: (9) / MARY'S SON (8) / AND GOD'S (7) / IS BORN! (6) / JESUS (5) / CAME (4) / FOR (3) / US! / (2) / REJOICE! (7).

Or perhaps: CHRISTMAS (9) / IS THE DAY (8) / ON WHICH (7) / THE SON (6) / OF GOD (5) / CAME (4) / FOR (3) / US (2), / JESUS! (5).

Some possible questions and answers for either of the above are:

1. What town was Jesus born in? (Bethlehem.)
2. In what kind of place was Jesus born? (In a stable.)
3. Why was Jesus born in a stable? (No room in the inn.)
4. Who were the first to hear of Jesus' birth? (The shepherds.)
5. Who announced Jesus' birth? (The angels.)
6. What two titles did the angels give to Jesus? (Messiah and Lord.)
7. What is another name for Messiah? (Christ, "the Anointed One.")
8. What song did the angels sing? ("Glory to God in the highest, and on earth peace to those on whom his favor rests" [Lk 2:14].)
9. Where were the shepherds minding their sheep? (In the fields.)
10. What family did Mary and Joseph belong to? (The family of David.)

If the theme message is about Easter, it might read: JESUS ROSE (9) / ON EASTER (8) / TO PROVE (7) / THAT HE (6) / IS THE (5) / ONLY (4) / SON (3) / OF (2) / GOD (3).

The possible questions and answers might be:

1. When did Jesus die? (Good Friday.)
2. How did Jesus die? (He was crucified.)
3. Why was Jesus crucified? (He claimed to be the Son of God.)
4. Where was Jesus buried? (In Joseph of Arimathea's tomb.)
5. On what day did Jesus rise? (Easter Sunday.)
6. How long was Jesus in the tomb? (Three days.)

7. To whom did Jesus appear first? (Mary Magdalene.)
8. Which apostle saw Jesus first after He rose? (Peter.)
9. Where did Jesus appear to His apostles? (In the upper room.)
10. What did Jesus' resurrection prove? (That He is truly the Son of God.)

From these examples, you can work out other phrases for other feasts. Since each of these starts with a nine-letter word, you will need to make up ten matching sets of cards bearing either statements or questions about the feast. If the first line has seven letters, you will need eight matching sets of questions or statements, and so on.

To offer you one last example, one that you might use to celebrate the anniversary of a priest, religious, principal, or so on, let me show you what I worked out for the celebration of the anniversary of profession for the Marist Brothers at their summer camp. (The feast is that of St. Anne, July 26.)

The theme message was: WE CELEBRATE (11) / THE DAY WHEN (10) / MANY OF THE (9) / BROTHERS (8) / OFFERED (7) / TO LIVE (6) / 3 VOWS (5) / MADE (4) / FOR (3) / US (2) / TO GOD (5).

Because there were 11 letters in the first word of the theme message, I needed 12 questions. The questions were:

1. Who began the Marist Brothers?
2. How many Marist Brothers are there?
3. Do the Brothers run their own schools?
4. How do you become a Marist Brother?
5. What is the vow of poverty?
6. What is the vow of chastity?
7. What is the vow of obedience?
8. How long does a man stay a Marist Brother?
9. What do Marist Brothers do?
10. Who takes care of the Marist Brothers?
11. Do Marist Brothers get married?
12. How can I share in the Marist Brothers' ministry?

So as you can see, this device can find a number of applications, with the challenge being to construct the theme message in the numerical order required, and then come up with suitable questions, always one more than the letters in the first word of the theme message.

Final Observations

There are five benefits of this presentation device:

1. While there is a magic trick involved, absolutely no skill is required. Moreover, it should not be presented as a trick but as a teaching device.
2. However, the magical element sustains attention right to the very end, because there is continuing interest to see if the cards on top of each pile will match.
3. The theme can be changed to suit whatever lesson one wants to teach.
4. Since the theme or subject matter can be changed, the method can be used from time to time without losing interest.
5. As I can personally attest, this method works just as well with adults as with children. However, for adults, you might want to make the questions a bit more sophisticated.

I hope you will take the time to work with this because it will add a dimension of "magic" to your presentation, which will fascinate both adults and children while leaving you free to concentrate on the presentation and getting your message across.

15

Surprise Gifts

(Epiphany)

The story of the Epiphany is one that easily captures the attention of those listening. It is filled with interesting, even mysterious, people from far-off lands; a miraculous star; a wondrous scene at the house of Jesus, Mary, and Joseph; unique gifts; and then the intrigue of secret messages to help the Magi evade the jealous, wicked King Herod. But, from all of this, what message do we want to give to the children? That challenge resulted in this homily, which focused on the three gifts — not so much because of their symbolism but because they were so unusual.

PROPS

The three gifts of the Magi should be visible from the beginning, perhaps on a table in front of the altar. They can be depicted in several ways according to your creativity. For example:

- **Gold**. A box covered with gold paper, or one that looks like a treasure chest in which are placed chocolate coins wrapped in gold foil, or checkers similarly wrapped to look like gold coins.
- **Frankincense**. The incense boat from the sacristy, unless you want something fancier.
- **Myrrh**. Some kind of vase or urn that might contain myrrh — that is, it looks somehow exotic and Eastern. (A trip to your local Pier 1 Imports store can probably provide these first three items.)
- **Surprise Gifts**. These should be out of sight or at least in Christmas boxes so as not to be seen until they are shown one at a time. They should be gifts you have received that are things you did not ask for or expect. I used a quilted Christmas throw blanket; some beautifully decorated Christmas stockings; a delightful pop-up book about Christmas; a marionette of a magician, the face of which looked like

me (!); a small and simple felt banner reading, *"Hodie Christus Natus Est,"* given to me by a high school student in my teaching days; and one or two other such items.

What you use will depend on your imagination — and the imaginations of those who have given you gifts!

HOMILY

Begin by asking the children to think of the gifts they received on Christmas, not the ones they asked for and expected to get, but those that were a complete surprise. Comment on how much fun it is to receive such a gift. Then hold up the three gifts of the Magi and suggest that these were surprise gifts, not the normal things to give to a young couple that have just had their first child. They needed diapers, a crib, clothes, formula, and maybe even a "donkey seat" for the baby!

Tell them that we have given these three gifts special meanings: the gold tells us Jesus is a King, the frankincense that He is God, and the myrrh that He will die. Explain briefly how the gifts show these ideas. Then go on to say that these were also very special surprise gifts because they were precious to the Magi who were happy to give them to the Holy Family.

Now show the gifts you received, and let the children react to them. This will bring home the idea that these things are truly "surprise" gifts. Then suggest that they can give surprise gifts to the members of their family, and not just at Christmas but throughout the year. These are gifts that will cost them little or no money, but will mean a lot to the person who receives them.

At this point, ask the children to think of such gifts and to tell you what they are. Begin by asking what they could do for their mom. After they have given some ideas, then ask about their dad. Next would be their siblings, and perhaps you could conclude with a surprise gift for their teacher. Depending on the children, these could be things such as making their bed, cleaning up their room, clearing the table and doing the dishes, taking out the garbage without being asked, doing *all* their homework every night, sharing their toys with their siblings, or trying to avoid fights with them. Then bring the whole homily to a conclusion by reviewing once more the idea of surprise gifts and suggesting that each of them should try to give at least one such gift that very day – and every day.

A Final Thought

You might emphasize the idea of the gifts that cost us nothing but time and love by making a large and fancy "Gift Certificate" on a poster board or piece of foam core. Leave blank the place for the "Recipient's Name" and the place for the "Gift." You can either point to these as you name the recipient and the gift, or perhaps even fill them out for the first example. This kind of visual aid will make clearer the idea you have only expressed in words.

16

Locket of Love

(St. Valentine's Day, Multipurpose Teaching Device)

This talk was given on or near St. Valentine's Day. The title came from a conversation I had with a very good friend who was telling of how her husband, the day after he met her, presented her with a gold locket, saying, "Some day I'm going to marry you" – and he did! Looking for some way to speak to the children about what love really means, I hit on the idea of using the story of the Locket of Love.

PROPS

I used a very simple method to teach the children various meanings of love. The device was a poster board (or oak tag, as it sometimes called), on which were written the words "**LOCKET OF LOVE**" *vertically*. Print the letters down the board with a series of dashes following each letter, the number of dashes equaling the number of letters needed to complete the word you are looking for. You will need an erasable marker to complete the words and an easel on which to rest the poster board.

HOMILY

I began by showing the children the actual locket, which I had borrowed from the lady for the occasion, and then telling them the story of how she got it. The goal was to elicit from the children a series of words that told us about what love really means. Then I brought the poster board forward (it was on an easel). As you will see, there are many thoughts about the various aspects of love that can be spoken about.

The first word is shown this way: **L** _ _ _ _ _ . The word filled in was L I S T E N. "We show that we love our parents or teachers when we LISTEN."

The words shown are the ones I used; you can use any words you wish as long as they give examples of real love and begin with the letters in the words "LOCKET OF LOVE," or a similar theme you may choose. The words in the parenthesis following the principal word should give the idea of love you are trying to get across to the children. Here's how the poster board looked when filled in:

L I S T E N (when your parents speak to you)
O B E Y (promptly)
C O O P E R A T E (with the rest of your family)
K I N D N E S S (to others brings kindness to you)
E X C U S E (the faults of others as you want to be excused)
T R U T H F U L N E S S (in all conversations)

O T H E R S (Love others as you want others to love you!)
F U N (Share good times with others!)

L E N D (Share the things you have with others!)
O R D E R (Keep your room in order!)
V I R T U E (Love is the most important of all the virtues!)
E V E R Y O N E (Love all, no matter who they are!)

As you can see, the words are not all the same part of speech (e.g., all nouns, all verbs), but the idea is to get as many signs of love as possible, starting with the letters in the three words "LOCKET OF LOVE," or your own expression of the theme. Don't be surprised if the children come up with words other than the ones above – and if they do, go with them! That way they feel really a part of the project, and not just as people trying to solve a puzzle or "to get the right answers." They'll spend enough time doing that for the rest of their lives!

A Next-to-Last Thought

A small group of people (usually parents) will want to help you in whatever way they can with your children's homilies, and you should use them whenever you can. For this particular homily, I asked them to make a Locket of Love for each child to take home after the Mass. The locket consisted of a little red heart (cut from construction paper or bought at a party store) fastened to a loop of red gift-wrapping ribbon (not the satin, but the paper ribbon). The committee enjoyed doing this (always try to give them enough lead time so that it will be fun and not a frantic last-minute chore), and the kids enjoyed having something pretty to take home with them. It also served the children as a reminder of what they had learned that day in the homily.

A Final Thought

This device of listing the first letter of a word or words and having the children fill in the remaining letters can be applied to all sorts of subjects: other virtues, names of Bible personalities, phrases or key words used by Jesus, and so on. So when you can't think of something more creative, this method is fairly easy to use. Just don't overuse it, or the novelty and fun will wear thin.

17

A Tale of Two Kings

(Christ the King, Lent, Palm Sunday)

This homily was fashioned for the celebration of the feast of Christ the King. If I may be so bold, I found this to be the most powerful of all the homilies in this book, from the point of view of the instant impact on the assembly. I hoped it would "play well," but I never expected it to have the impact it did. It also taught me once again how much more powerful the visual presentation is over the merely verbal.

PROPS

1. A rather large cardboard box covered with gold wrapping paper, to which are affixed large cutout diamonds or round-shaped pieces of brightly colored construction paper. These cutouts represent "jewels" on the "gold" box. The box should be of such size as to hold:
    (a) A square yard of inexpensive red material with Velcro fasteners at adjacent corners to make it a child's cape.
    (b) A crown (easily purchased at a party-supply or card shop).
    (c) A king's scepter. I purchased one at a party shop.
2. An obviously well-worn cloth bag containing:
    (a) A square yard of inexpensive purple material, also with Velcro fasteners at adjacent corners, to make it a child's cape.
    (b) A crown of thorns — actually a wreath made of branches, which can be purchased at a flower shop or garden nursery. It should be of such size as to fit comfortably on a child's head.
    (c) A reed plucked from anywhere reeds grow, or a similar piece obtained from a florist.

These props may take a little work to gather, but believe me, the visual effect they have and the impact of the message they teach will be well worth the effort.

Begin by telling the children you are going to talk about kings – not bad kings, but good kings. Ask them to tell you what a king does. This can lead to some startling answers, but that's okay; the kids are involved, and if they come up with humorous answers, so much the better. It will hold their attention and that of their parents. Never forget that the parents are there to learn from the homily, too.

After you have established that kings are people who rule others, live in castles, wear crowns, etc., then develop the idea that they also care for those over whom they rule, giving them food at times of famine and shelter at times of attack, and so on. Remember, we're talking about *good* kings.

Now, select a boy to be a king. Ask the rest of the children what he needs to show that he is a king. Of course, the items he needs are those in the gold box – plus a "throne," so have a chair handy for him to sit on. Then, as each item is mentioned (the cape, the crown, and the scepter), remove it from the box and place it on the boy – or in the case of the scepter, in his hand.

Next, select another boy and have him stand near the first one, who is now dressed as a king. Bring out the cloth bag and, without asking the questions about what he needs, say, "This king also has a cape [put the violet cape around his shoulders], a crown [put the "crown of thorns" on his head], and a scepter [put the reed into his hand]."

The contrast will be startling, as I learned the first time I did this.

Actually, I had a longer homily planned, but the laughter and comments coming from or being passed among the adults who were responding to the humorous remarks and the dressing up of the boy-kings indicated nothing of what was about to happen. In just the few moments it took me to dress the second boy in the purple cape, the crown of thorns, and the reed, a sudden silence came over the entire church as the people realized they were looking at the contrast of an earthly king and Christ the King during His Passion. I immediately sensed that the best thing to do was "wrap it up" as quickly as possible, letting the visual image speak for itself. So this is what I did: Standing next to the first king, I said, "This king died and was buried, and the crown, robe, and scepter were put back into the gold box." As I spoke these words, I removed these items from the first boy, placed them into the gold box, and — quietly thanking the boy for his help — sent him back to his place.

Then, standing behind the Christ figure, I continued: "This king died, too, and was buried, and the crown and robe and scepter were thrown back into the old, worn bag." (Do this as you speak, then put the bag aside, and have the boy return to his place.) "But a wonderful thing happened. This second King came back to life three days after He died, and now He is King of all the heavens and all the earth. That is the wonderful King we honor and worship today, Jesus Christ, our Risen King. (You may embellish this as you see fit, but be very careful of over-kill. The visual message is *very powerful,* believe me!)

In our church, we have the figure of the Resurrected Christ on the cross over the main altar, so I was able to point to that while speaking of the King who came back to life. If you have this situation, then let it work for you. If you don't, perhaps you could bring to the sanctuary that day a crucifix bearing the corpus of the Resurrected Christ. While this is not necessary for the success of the homily, it should help.

18

Easter Eggs and 'Alleluia!'

(Easter Season)

This homily can work wonderfully well, not only on Easter Sunday but also on one of the Sundays during the Easter season. Special children's homilies on Easter Sunday, when the church is so crowded, may play havoc with the parking lot and the "turnaround time" needed between Masses. But you're going to give a homily anyway, so why not a children's homily? It might just bring some of the "hearty annuals" (and their children) back the next week! On the other hand, using this homily on one of the Sundays during the Easter season (as I have done when Easter is not on the "Family Mass" Sunday) emphasizes the fact that the Church celebrates Easter for 50 days, not just one, so take your pick.

PROPS

1. Several different kinds of eggs: a real one (handle with care!), a wooden one (found in toy shops), a candy one (usually chocolate at Easter time), a ceramic one or polished stone egg (found in gift shops), one or two actual Easter eggs, and most importantly, a plastic egg that comes apart in the middle. The latter is available in a variety of colors during the pre-Easter season in party, toy, and card shops. Try to find the largest one possible. If you wish, this one can be decorated as an Easter egg. I have also found even larger cardboard eggs (usually filled with candy) decorated with foil. These work very well for the "main" egg.
2. A basket large enough to hold all the eggs.
3. A glass into which you break the real egg after displaying it to show it is real.
4. A strip of paper on which are written the words "**JESUS IS RISEN!**" Make this as bright as possible, but it cannot be any wider than the length of the large plastic egg that comes apart. This strip will be

rolled up tightly and placed inside the large plastic egg. It is the last egg produced.

5. A strip of poster board, 8" x 28". On this are printed the words **"PRAISE TO GOD."**

6. A strip of poster board, 8" x 14", on which is printed the word **"HALLEL."** This piece is creased vertically through the "H" so that, when folded to the front, the "H" is no longer seen. (See illustration.)

7. A similar strip, 8" x 14", on which is printed the word "**JAHWEH.**" This piece is creased so that the "WEH" part, when folded toward the front, shows an exclamation point. (See illustration.)

8. A piece of poster board, 8" x 4", on which is printed the letter "**U.**" As you can see, the lengths of the three pieces add up to 32". They are to be hinged onto the "PRAISE TO GOD" piece *at the top* so that the three pieces, laid next to one another, hang down over and extend at either end beyond the "PRAISE" piece. If properly placed, "HALLEL" should cover the word "PRAISE," the "U" should cover the word "TO," and "JAHWEH" should cover the word "GOD." The text of the homily will make clear the reason for this arrangement and how far they should extend. (See illustration.)

9. A piece of paper on which are written six questions, in response to which members of the assembly are to profess their faith and renew their baptismal promises as they do every Easter. This should be on the altar where it can be picked up easily.

This homily actually has two parts; either part could be used alone. However, when used together, they make a very strong impact, as I will show at the end.

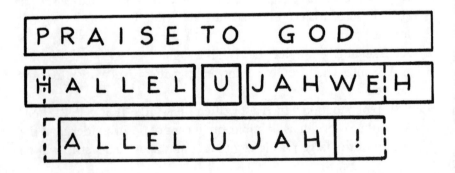

Begin the homily by asking the children to tell you what one very special word is connected with the feast of Easter, a word they haven't heard on Sunday since the beginning of Lent. Almost immediately one of them will say, "Alleluia!" Ask them if they know where the word comes from and what it means. The chances are very good that no one will know.

Bring out the card with the flaps. Explain to them that our word "ALLELUIA" comes from three Hebrew words, and that Hebrew is the language of the Jewish people. The first word is "HALLEL," which means "PRAISE." Point to the word, and have the children repeat it after you. Then show them the word "JAHWEH," and tell them it means "GOD" or "THE LORD." Have them also repeat this word.

Finally, point to the middle word – "U" – and tell them it is a Hebrew word meaning "TO." (This is stretching it a bit.)

Now have them read these three words all together two or three times; it comes out "HALLEL-U-JAHWEH." Now, fold back the "H" from "HALLEL" and the "WEH" from "JAHWEH," and they will see "ALLELUJAH!" (As noted above, these two flaps should be creased vertically before you start, so as to make this folding back easy to do. If you wish, you can have a paper clip at the top of each flap so that you can clip it closed when it is folded over.)

Have them say "ALLELUJAH!" three times, and then lift the three pieces, one at a time, to reveal the words "PRAISE TO GOD." Let them say this three times. Then ask three times, "What does Allelujah (Alleluia) mean?" and they will respond, "Praise to God!" Now hand this sign off to a server (who should stand off to the side), but keep the sign in sight. You will need it. So much for the first part.

Begin the second half of the homily by asking the children to tell you what one of the most popular *symbols* of Easter is. They may mention the bunny, or even the butterfly, but surely some of them will name the egg. Bring out the basket and show them the various eggs it contains, one at a time. Explain how they are different from one another.

Before you bring out the last egg – the large plastic egg (or the even larger cardboard, foil-covered egg) containing the strip that says "JESUS IS RISEN" – ask them *why* the egg is a symbol of Easter. Some of them will be able to tell you it represents the tomb; and just as the chicken comes out with new life, so Jesus came out from the tomb with new life. (Some of the children will have learned this in school or religion class. If not, *tell them about it!*)

To illustrate this, separate the two halves of the large egg, revealing the rolled-up paper. Slowly unroll it, and ask them to read what it says. The older ones will have no trouble with this, and the younger ones will be excited at seeing it and hearing it read to them.

Now bring this presentation to a rousing climax of real vocal celebration. Ask them, "What does 'Alleluia!' mean?" and they will respond, "Praise to God!" and you immediately ask, "And why do we say, 'Praise to God'?" Hold up the scroll with the words "JESUS IS RISEN!" and have them read those words aloud. Do that two or three more times, asking them to say it louder each time. You will be amazed at how enthusiastic they will get.

For the "rousing climax" mentioned above, tell the children to stand up and continue to cheer, "Jesus is risen! Praise to God!" Then ask everyone in the church to do the same — and they will! I did this spontaneously the first time I ever used this homily, and the adults got as vocally excited as the kids did. There were a thousand Catholics standing on their feet and proclaiming our central teaching, and they were excited about it! Maybe for the first time they began to understand the excitement that should fill our hearts on Easter and throughout the season. (*And* **please** *don't worry about those few who will comment negatively on the idea of everyone standing and cheering for the Lord. They simply don't understand what a* **real** *celebration is all about!*)

Then for a *really* exciting finish to this Easter homily, have on the altar the sheet of paper on which are written the six questions that we ask the assembly every Easter when we profess our faith and renew our baptismal vows. If you sense that the assembly is really "with you," then finish by saying with great enthusiasm, "Now while you're all standing and cheering for the Lord, I have some questions for you."

Skipping the introduction given in the Sacramentary, go right into them, proclaiming those questions and building on the enthusiasm and excitement you (and the Holy Spirit!) have just created. You and your people will experience probably the most fervent expression of faith in the Risen Jesus in which you have ever participated.

This may sound like an evangelical tent meeting, but what's wrong with that? Aren't we supposed to be, in the words of Pope John Paul II, "an Easter people, with 'Alleluia' as [our] song"? Then let's show it by getting excited about it, especially on this greatest of all feasts!

19

Easter Butterfly

(Easter Season, Resurrection, New Life)

This homily found its origin in one of the earliest of all Christian symbols, the butterfly. The image of the beautiful butterfly emerging from its cocoon was one easily adopted to represent Jesus emerging to new life from the tomb. It is also an image that little children can understand and perhaps even recall from a parish school lesson or CCD class.

PROPS

In my original presentation, I used a magic prop and therefore was reluctant to include this homily in this collection. However, it can be done just as effectively by using the paper bag described in Chapter 5, "It's Cleanup Time!" (see pages 32-33). You may recall that it was a paper bag (sack) prepared in such fashion as to have it contain two compartments, front and back; and once the contents of the front section were removed, it could be torn open to be shown "empty."

For this Easter homily, you might want to decorate the bag to resemble a tomb by using a heavy black felt pen to draw lines on it resembling stones of a tomb. You could also label it "Joseph's Tomb," giving you the opportunity to tell the children how Jesus was so poor that He was buried in someone else's tomb. You can also comment on how generous Joseph of Arimathea was by giving his tomb to bury Jesus. The "tomb" should be out of sight as the homily begins, but readily accessible.

You will need four handkerchiefs, scarves, or pieces of material about 18" square (each of a different color: green, red, blue, and yellow). On each of these should be fastened a black felt cutout of a caterpillar. (See illustration.) These should be fastened to the material with a slight touch of spray mount, available from any art store. It is a spray rubber cement and, when lightly applied, will do no harm to the fabric.

The final piece of material will provide another opportunity to involve the volunteer services of a parish artist. You will need a piece of material 36" square. It can be any color, or even black or white. On it, paint or draw a butterfly using the four colors of the scarves. (See illustration.) This butterfly scarf goes in the *front* compartment of the "tomb" (bag). Whatever fabric you use, make it as lightweight as possible so that it doesn't bulge in the bag.

(If you would prefer to get these items "ready-made," I suggest that you purchase them at a local magic shop. If there is none near you, contact either P&A Silks [P.O. Box 651, Hudson, NY 12534; phone 1-518-537-4616] or Laflin's Magic and Silks [P.O. Box 228, Sterling, CO 80751; 1-303-522-2589]. Either of these firms should be able to provide the four scarves mentioned and the butterfly scarf. Just be sure that the four colors of the silks [as magicians call scarves] are also found on the butterfly scarf. These will not be inexpensive, but the effect of this presentation and the impact it makes will be well worth it.)

This homily can also be used in any presentation of the Resurrection for your school or CCD classes, so you should get more than one use out of it. You can also use it every other Easter season.

The final item needed is a 36"-square piece of foam core. Using erasable markers, divide it into four 18" squares by outlining those squares on the foam core using the four colors that correspond to the scarves. The upper-left one should be green, the upper-right red, the lower-left blue, and the lower-right yellow (but call it "gold").

In the green box, print in green letters "**JESUS GIVES US LIFE**." In the red box, print in red letters "**JESUS GIVES US LOVE**." In the blue box, print in blue letters "**JESUS KEEPS HIS PROMISES**." And in the yellow (gold) box, print in yellow letters "**JESUS IS GOD**."

Finally, using pushpins, fasten the four scarves (bearing the felt caterpillars) over their respective matching colored squares. I realize this is a lot of preparation, but I think you will find the effort well worth it.

HOMILY

The secret to this presentation is to stress the colors and what they stand for. The one thing you don't want people saying as they leave is, "How did he do that?" The little bit of magic should *contribute* to the presentation but *never* overshadow it.

Begin by having the foam core (with the scarves attached) carried in the Opening Procession and placed on an easel at the side of the sanctuary, opposite the ambo and Paschal candle. (Nothing should distract from the candle.) When homily time comes, and while the children are taking their places in front of the altar, bring the easel forward. (There will probably be lots of flowers in front of the altar – after all, it is the Easter season! So you can either place the easel to the side of the altar or have some of the plants removed just before the Mass so that the easel can be placed in front of the altar.)

Going to the easel, point to the four scarves and ask, one by one, what the children think the colors stand for. The green should tell us of *hope* or *new life*, the red should tell us of *love*, the blue about *loyalty* ("true blue"), and the gold (yellow) about *the most precious metal we have*.

Also, ask them what the black figure on each scarf is. They will tell you it is a caterpillar. Then ask what becomes of the caterpillar when it wraps itself in a cocoon. Some of them will be able to tell you it comes out as a butterfly.

Now one by one, remove the scarves, taking time to read what is written on the square it covered. As each scarf is removed, call a child forward and have him/her hold the scarf by the top corners in front of himself/herself. Once more, review the colors and their meaning using the words on the board. Now ask, "Which of these four statements about Jesus is the most important?" The answer, of course, is "JESUS IS GOD" (gold/yellow). To emphasize this, remove the caterpillars from the other three scarves and put them aside.

Here introduce the "tomb," stating briefly that in the past few days we have been celebrating the most wonderful days in the history of the world, those days on which Jesus gave us himself in Holy Communion, then died for us on the cross, and then rose again from the dead. He is just like a butterfly that comes out of the cocoon into a whole new life.

Take the four scarves from the children, one at a time, and drop them into the *rear* compartment of the "tomb." This is facilitated by pinching closed the top of the front and middle sections of the bag. (As you take each child's scarf, ask him/her to resume his/her seat.) The yellow (gold) one still bearing the caterpillar should go in last. Tell them this represents Jesus being buried after He died on the cross.

But three days later, He came out from the tomb, just like a butterfly! Pinching closed the middle and back panels of the bag, reach into the *front* compartment of the "tomb," and take out the butterfly scarf. Put the bag aside — but still in view — and display the beautiful butterfly scarf. Be sure to point out the four colors in the butterfly, asking again what they stand for. (Remember, you want to stress those four very important attributes of Jesus.) Then, using the pushpins already on the foam core, fasten the butterfly scarf to the foam core, and leave it on the easel for the rest of the Mass. You may even want to have it carried out during the Recessional.

Finally, to satisfy those who will surely be asking, "Let's see what's in the 'tomb' [bag]," pick it up and hold it in full view. Then ask, "And how do we know that Jesus truly rose from the dead?" As you answer your own question (unless one of the children beats you to it!), say, "The tomb was empty!" Then, pinching the middle and back panels together, tear the front of the "tomb" open, showing it to be "empty." This will really sell the whole idea of Jesus rising from the dead — and might even bring a round of applause!

I realize that this homily calls for more preparation than most of the others (and some expense, too). But as noted, you will find that it is well worth it. If you do it on Easter or Passion (Palm) Sunday, you will reach many people who only come those days, and you might just lead them to think about coming back more regularly. A homily like this can do such things! Besides, it is the feast of the Lord's resurrection, and whatever we do should genuinely contribute to the color and excitement of the celebration. So celebrate!

(A final thought: Remembering that we should keep celebrating for all the 50 days of the Easter season, feel free to use this on *any* of the Sundays during this season.)

20

We Are His Light in the World

(Ascension)

What does one do to teach children about the Ascension of Jesus? It can be difficult enough to teach this mystery to adults, but how to share it with children? In this case, let me offer two approaches. (By the way, both of these would be more suited to school-age children than for those younger. You will see why as we go through them.)

In this first homily on the Ascension, we want to teach the lesson that Jesus lives on in us even after He has ascended to the right hand of the Father. So what better way than to use one of the most powerful visuals (in my opinion, second only to the crucifix) that the Church gives us? I am speaking about the Paschal candle. The whole ceremony of the Easter Vigil that centers around *the* sign of the Risen Jesus — the Paschal candle — is a classic example of visual teaching. Let's use it again, therefore, to teach the mystery of God's abiding presence within and among us.

PROPS

The visual aids needed here are few and simply acquired: the Paschal candle and sufficient Vigil tapers, so that there is one for each of the children (and adults) present. These should be distributed as the children enter. Since the tapers will be lit during the homily, their distribution should be age-appropriate.

This homily works best within a situation where the church lights can be turned off easily, thus making the impact of the candles all the stronger.

(**CAUTION:** This homily requires that the Paschal candle be extinguished during the homily. Since the Church has moved the extinguishing of the candle from the Ascension to the feast of Pentecost, you may not wish to use this presentation during a seasonal Mass. On the other hand, the fact that you extinguish it during the homily on Ascension Thursday [or the Sunday following], just to make your point, doesn't mean it can't be relighted after the homily. Moreover, this certainly could be used effectively at a paraliturgy during the season or during one on baptism.)

HOMILY

Begin by pointing out the important role the Paschal candle plays in our Easter liturgy and throughout the year at baptisms and funerals. Stress that it is lit at the Easter Vigil and stands for Jesus rising from the dead, to spread the joy of His light to all the world. You might even describe in some detail the solemn lighting of the candle, the Procession, its being incensed, and the singing of the beautiful song to the candle ("The Exsultet") to underline its importance. (Most of the children will not have seen the Vigil ceremony, but it is hoped they will have noticed the lighted Paschal candle during the liturgies of the Easter season.) Jesus calls himself "the light of the world," but He also calls *us* "the light of the world." So how are we to be this light?

At this point, ask all those who were given a candle to pick it up and hold it in their hand. When this is accomplished, talk about Jesus leaving us to return to the Father in heaven, to receive His reward for doing so well His job of saving us. But Jesus wants us to continue His work. That, after all, is why we are called to be Christians — to be Christ to all the people we meet. So before Jesus left to go to heaven, He gave us His light, His life, that wonderful gift we call *grace* (which I always define as "God living in and through me").

At this point, turn off the lights in the church, making it as dark as possible. This shows the Paschal candle as the only source of light in the building. Now take your taper, light it from the Paschal candle, and begin to light the tapers of those people in the sanctuary and then those of the people in the first row. Send some of the ministers from the sanctuary to light tapers in various areas of the church, asking all those present to "pass it on," just as is done at the Vigil.

When everyone's taper is lit, call attention once more to the Paschal candle, and then blow or snuff it out. This leaves the church still bathed in light, but now it is from the tapers of all those present.

The message is clear: *Though Jesus is no longer visible in our midst, He is present in each one of us, and we must make Him visible by bringing the message of Jesus to the world.* Add the fact that when each of us was baptized, our godfather was given a candle that was also lit from the Paschal candle. This was a sign of our receiving God's life into our souls so that we could share it with others.

Finally, turn the church lights on, and tell those holding the tapers to extinguish them. (Be sure to remind them to let the wax harden before they put their candles down. The pastor will certainly appreciate their thoughtfulness!) Conclude by restating the message: Though Jesus may no longer be visibly present in the world, He is certainly present in each one of us. Our role is to make that presence visible.

21

We Become Signs of Jesus

(Sacraments, Ascension)

The message here is similar to "Jesus ascended but is still with us." However, the medium of instruction here will be the seven sacraments; hence, it is suitable only for school-age children. The message is that although Jesus is no longer visibly present in our midst, He still continues to minister to His people through the sacraments.

This presentation will involve seven children (are you surprised?) as "sign holders." They should be called from the assembly one at a time. If all seven are gathered at the beginning of the homily, the last ones to be put into service can become fidgety and distract from what you are trying to accomplish.

PROPS

Seven pieces of poster board, 22" x 14" each (half-sheets), on which there will be printing on both sides. They can all be of the same color; or if you want to enhance the appearance of the presentation, they can be of seven different colors. (For economy, I suggest that they all be of the same color. Moreover, the same color on each sign causes no distraction that could possibly result from using a variety of colors.)

The signs should read:

Side One	Side Two
(1) **GAVE NEW LIFE**	BAPTISM
(2) **FORGAVE SINS**	RECONCILIATION
(3) **DIED AND ROSE AGAIN**	EUCHARIST
(4) **SENT THE HOLY SPIRIT**	CONFIRMATION
(5) **HEALED THE SICK**	ANOINTING OF THE SICK
(6) **LOVED US**	MARRIAGE
(7) **SENT MEN TO TEACH**	PRIESTHOOD

The signs should be printed with the words on one side right side up and the other side upside down. This makes it easier for the children to simply flip the card over when they are told to do so, rather than having to turn it around, end to end, which some do not do easily.

HOMILY

Begin by asking the children to think about all the things Jesus did while He was on earth – the really important things. Then ask them to begin to tell you some of those things. The best way to keep them from coming up with responses you don't want is to ask them "leading questions." That way you control the flow of answers without seeming to put down any of the children by rejecting their answers.

Please note that it is *not* important to get the sacraments listed in order. The idea is to have the children see the connection between the actions of Jesus while He was on earth and the actions of Jesus as they are continued in the sacraments.

For example, some leading questions might be:

Q. What good thing did Jesus do very often during His life?
A. **He healed the sick.**

Call the first child forward and ask him/her to hold the sign that says "HEALED THE SICK" so that those words are facing the assembly.

Q. What did Jesus often do at the same time He healed people from their illnesses?
A. **He forgave sins.**

The second child is called up to hold that sign.

Q. What is the most important thing Jesus ever did?
A. **He died and rose again.**

The third child gets this sign.

Q. Before Jesus went back to heaven, He promised to send some-one special. Who was that special someone?

A. **He sent the Holy Spirit.**

The fourth child gets that sign.

Q. How did Jesus make sure we would hear His message?

A. **He sent men to teach.**

The fifth child gets that sign.

Q. Besides the Eucharist, what is the most precious gift Jesus gave to us?

A. **He gave us new life.**

(You may have to work on this one — perhaps tell of the time when Jesus said, "I came so that they might have life" [Jn 10:10].)

The sixth child gets that sign.

Q. Why did God the Father send Jesus to save us?

A. **He loves us.**

The seventh child gets that sign.

Now that you have the seven children holding the seven signs, you speak about how Jesus wanted His work to continue, even though He was going back to the Father. To do this, He gave us seven signs — or ways — in which His work could be carried on. Let's see what those signs are.

Here you go to the first one that was called out: "HEALED THE SICK." Point to it and ask the child holding it to turn the sign over. He/she will flip it over and the assembly will see "ANOINTING OF THE SICK." Talk a little about that — about how Jesus heals the sick in spirit, and sometimes even those who are physically sick — and then move on to the next sign. Continue until the names of all seven sacraments are showing.

Conclude by reviewing how the most important things that Jesus did while He was on earth are still being done through *us*. Again, this can be developed according to the age and knowledge of the children. This review does two things: (1) it teaches them that although Jesus ascended to the Father in heaven, He still continues His work among us, and (2) it teaches them that the sacraments are more than ceremonies, that they are the very actions of Jesus himself in today's world.

When you come to the Sacrament of Marriage, explain that when a man and woman get married, they are to try from then on to love each other so totally, so beautifully, that their love will become a sign of God's love in our lives. **This is a concept that is all too often not taught, but it is the main reason behind the love of man and woman being made into a sacrament. The couple are to be to all of us a sign of God's love.**

(**CAUTION:** It may take some additional "leading" questions to get the answers you want, *but give the children time to come up with the answers.* Don't be too anxious and therefore supply the correct answer before the children can. Get them to *think!*)

An Added Thought

If the children are of upper primary or middle grades, this is a very good time to introduce them to a teaching that is often neglected in *all* our sacramental presentations — namely, that we must do more than *receive* the sacraments; we must *become* the sacraments. By that we mean that *we* are to become the signs of Jesus ministering to His people today by the way we minister to one another. Thus, if we are forgiven our sins, we must then be signs of that forgiveness by forgiving others. Again, we receive Holy Communion not only for ourselves as a sign of God's love for us, but also so that we can show God's love is present in the way we love one another. This aspect of our sacramental theology needs to be stressed in order for our people, both children and adults, to come to a deeper knowledge and appreciation of the fundamental role that the sacraments are to play in our lives and the role we are to play in the lives of others.

22

The Spirit in the Wind

(Holy Spirit, Pentecost, Confirmation, Virtues)

While I know that there are other signs of the Holy Spirit, most notably the tongues of fire and the dove, the sign that has always made the greatest impact on me is that of the wind. When the Spirit came on the first Pentecost, the initial sign of His presence was the terrible wind that shook the whole house where the apostles were. Moreover, because we cannot see the wind but we certainly see or feel its effects, it seems to me a very powerful sign or symbol of the presence of the Holy Spirit. With this in mind, I developed what is essentially a simple presentation, consisting mostly of pictures, but one that I found helped the little children to understand something about the presence and effect of the Holy Spirit in their lives.

PROPS

Four pieces of poster board on which are drawn the following images (one on each poster): a flag flying in the breeze, a kite aloft in the sky, a sailboat with sail out full, and clouds blowing across the sky. (Additional optional images are listed at the end.)

HOMILY

Show the pictures, one at a time, to the children, asking them to simply try to remember what they see. When all four have been shown, ask them what the four pictures have in common. Usually, because they were not asked to look for a commonality, they will not discover it. This gives you the opportunity to show all four pictures again. This time someone will almost certainly say the thing they have in common is the wind.

Now point out (by showing the pictures individually) the role the wind plays in each one of these pictures. The flag and the kite could not fly, the sailboat could not move, and the clouds would stand still if it were not for the wind. So we can see the things the wind *does*, but we cannot see the wind itself. No one has ever seen it!

The same can be said of the Holy Spirit. No one has ever seen the Third Person of the Blessed Trinity, yet we believe in Him and have seen the effects of the Spirit's presence within us. From here on, the presentation is up to you, as are the examples you use to show the children what the Holy Spirit can do for them.

Some Suggestions

You might point out the love that their parents show for each other and their children, or the many good works that the children do for their parents. They can't *see* the love that is behind those good actions, but they certainly see the *effects* of their love in their good works. The same can be said of the love they have for their siblings and their friends, and perhaps for people they don't even know (e.g., those they help in a special project done for the homeless, the hungry, or the handicapped).

You can also speak of telling the truth, of obeying, of being kind, and of being forgiving and patient, none of which can be seen, but the effects of which are clearly obvious.

For older children, you could cite the courage of the martyrs, which was given by the Holy Spirit, and point out that courage is also invisible. But you can certainly see the effects of it in the way the martyrs gave up their lives to show their love for God.

None of these *virtues* — the word means "power" (i.e., God's power in them and in each one of us) — can be seen. But these powers come from the Holy Spirit, and like the Holy Spirit, we can certainly see the effects of them and Him.

Final Thoughts

Granted that some of these virtuous acts are hard to depict in a simple drawing, you may wish to use other images: a picture of a gift box; a sign reading "Soup Kitchen"; a photo (taken from a magazine) of a nice neat room; a picture of a TV set with nothing showing on the screen (Why? Because those who were watching went to the dinner table when they were called!); posters bearing the words "Please," "Thank you," "I'm sorry," "I forgive you," and similar ideas will help make clearer the message that the Holy Spirit does give us these wonderful powers, even if we can't see Him.

Conclude by reminding the children that they all received the Holy Spirit when they were baptized and will receive Him again in a special way when they receive confirmation. In this way, they can begin to reflect on what is admittedly a difficult concept, but one they (and their parents) must try to grasp if their prayer life is to make any progress at all.

23

The Mystery of the Trinity

(Holy Trinity, Sign of the Cross)

A homily on the Blessed Trinity can be challenging enough for adults; it is quite difficult for children. Yet, by using visuals, they can be given some idea of what the mystery means, and even come away with a lesson that applies to their young lives.

PROPS

The theme of this homily is *signs*; therefore, you will need several signs. The ones I use (as usual, you may choose your own if these don't suit you) are explained in the homily. They were made by pasting shapes made from construction paper onto poster board. Of course, they could be painted for you by that parish artist whose talents you have benefited from before!

HOMILY

Show an **EXIT** sign (red capital letters on black background). Explain that this sign uses a *word* to deliver the message. Ask them what the word EXIT means. You may be surprised how many children do not know, and you will teach them a valuable lesson in the asking!

Next, show a **STOP** sign. This is the usual red octagonal sign with the word printed in large, white capital letters. Show them the *back* side of it first; many will be able to identify it by its shape alone. Then turn it around to show the other children the word STOP. The STOP sign is a combination of the shape of the sign and the word.

A **HOSPITAL** sign. This uses just one letter: it is the white capital "**H**" in the center of a blue square or rectangle. By showing this, you also teach a valuable lesson the children might need sometime on a trip.

A **McDONALD'S** sign. This is simply the golden arches on a red background. This is now a universal sign that needs no words!

Finally, a **BARBER POLE** (i.e., the red and white striped pole). Announce that this is more for the adults, which keeps them involved. Probably one of the older children will be able to tell you what it signifies.

Having shown these signs, you will now move to the Blessed Trinity, for which there are three signs. Tell them that the Trinity means three Persons in one God, and that They are all equal.

Show them the **PERFECT TRIANGLE**. (I suggest you use yellow poster board for this.) This should be made of three equal sides with three equal angles and should not be a solid piece, but one that has a triangle cut out of the inner part. (See illustration.) In this way, they can see the three sides and the three angles quite clearly. Label the arms of the triangle "**FATHER**," "**SON**," and "**HOLY SPIRIT**." By revolving it three times, you can show that it looks the same no matter how you hold it. And the three Persons (whose names they see) are equal to one another no matter what position they are in. Explain that this was one of the first signs Catholics used to try to show the mystery of the Trinity.

Next comes the **SHAMROCK**. This should be quite large so that you can print the words "**HOLY TRINITY**" in the middle of the top or bottom side, and the names of the three Persons (one on each leaf). Explain the meaning of this: three leaves on one stem shows the three Persons in one God, and tell them that this was used by St. Patrick to teach the pagans in Ireland. (The shamrock — along with an illustration — is used in the next chapter.)

Finally, show them the **THREE INTERLOCKING RINGS**. These could all be the same color or three different colors — or if you want to get really fancy, make all three the same color on one side and three different colors on the other side by pasting different colored circles back to back. The different colors on one side show the uniqueness of each Person, but when put together and turned around, the circles all have the same color. These rings should be open in the middle (they are not three *discs* but three *rings*), and they should be large enough so that when they overlap you can see space between them. (See illustration.) To show this sign as a unit, use double-stick Scotch tape to join them into the traditional three interlocking rings. You might mention that this sign was used by St. Thomas Aquinas to try to depict the Trinity. (Should you be a magic hobbyist, this is a wonderful time to use the linking rings — but use only three of them!)

Now tell them there is one more sign of the Trinity that every Catholic should know. See if they can guess. It's the **SIGN OF THE CROSS**. (This could be a large brown cross on a green background.) Whether they know this or not, show it to them and then say that this is a very special prayer that every Catholic should know. Proceed to teach it to them, asking the older children to help the younger ones.

Begin by teaching them the words. Say them slowly and have the children repeat them. Do this three times.

Now teach them the gestures. Begin by making sure they are using their *right* hand. (You thereby teach the little ones something else that's new to many of them – which hand is the right hand!) I suggest that, as you do this, you turn your back to them, make the gestures as large as possible, and turn your head back over your shoulder to lead them in saying the words. The reason? If, while facing them, you gesture from your left shoulder to the right for "the Holy Spirit," you will find that they will move their hand from the right shoulder to the left, moving in the same direction as you do, as in a mirror. (This often happens in confession when the priest is giving absolution!)

Having taught them the Sign of the Cross, you can add one more lesson if you choose: *they* are to be the sign of the Blessed Trinity! When they make the sign on themselves, they make themselves into a sign of God's presence in the world. They do this by saying their prayers (beginning and ending with the Sign of the Cross), by being kind, loving, forgiving, and generous to all the members of their families and their friends. This is how we come to know more about the Blessed Trinity and how we show others that we believe God is always with us.

An Afterthought

I have also used this homily with older children (up to mid-teens), on which occasion I introduce two additional secular signs: the **SKIDDING MARKS** sign and the **NO SMOKING** sign. You can teach valuable moral lessons with these concerning the responsibility of driving slowly and carefully, and the need they have *not* to begin smoking. Then add two other Catholic signs or symbols that we don't see as often as in former days, but which still are quite visible in some places. I'm speaking of the **IHS** and the **CHI-RHO**. (It's also interesting to discover how many adults do not know what these mean.)

Two cards are required, each perhaps 22" x 14".

For the first card, on one side, draw the Greek letters "**IHS**." On the reverse side, put the three Greek letters, one under the other, with its English equivalent opposite:

$$I = J$$
$$H = E$$
$$S = S$$

It is immediately obvious that this is a sign from the earliest days of the Church for the name Jesus.

The second card should have the Chi-Rho sign on one side, and on the reverse side the Greek letters, one under the other, and the English equivalent opposite:

$$X = CH$$
$$P = R$$

Again, it becomes immediately obvious that this is a sign from the earliest days of the Church for the name Christ.

Whenever I use these additional cards, I ask if anyone knows what they mean. If no one does, I will suggest (anticipating their possible answers) that the first one does *not* mean "I hate school" or "I have suffered"! I then add that they are not initials, but letters in a word.

When you ask what the second sign means, don't be surprised if some of the youngsters tell you that it is a "No Parking" sign! They will confuse this with one of the international signs we have become so accustomed to, especially if you use one or more of them in the first part of this presentation. Tell them again it is a combination of two letters from a longer word. Then give the explanation.

Conclude with some thoughts on what they should be thinking about whenever they make and *pray* the Sign of the Cross.

24

Shamrocks

(Holy Trinity, St. Patrick's Day, Lent, Holy Family, Mass; Creed, Code, and Cult)

Since the patron saint of my parish is St. Patrick, from time to time I have had to provide a homily for the school children at the Feast Day Mass. However, this homily can be used in any parish on that feast because St. Patrick is known far and wide as one of the great evangelists of the Church. In addition, this feast always falls during Lent (March 17), and this homily addresses some of the chief aspects of that holy season. So one need not be Irish to use this homily; one need only be Christian!

PROPS

All you need for this homily are five large shamrocks (or more if you can think of additional three-fold themes) made out of poster board. (See illustration.) The ones I made are approximately 25" high and 25" wide. This produces three large leaves on each shamrock, on which you will write a number of different ideas. I suggest that in addition to the green one (of course!), you also make the others out of different colors. That way the different message on each shamrock will be highlighted with a different color.

On the green shamrock, print the words "**HOLY TRINITY**" on one side, and on the reverse side print the words "**FATHER**," "**SON**," and "**HOLY SPIRIT**" (one divine name on each leaf.) This will be the first shamrock, which will provide the opportunity to speak of how St. Patrick used the shamrock to teach the people of Ireland about the Holy Trinity. Present the remaining four shamrocks in whatever order agrees with the emphasis you want to place on each. The other themes I selected were:

- "**LENT**," with the reverse showing "**PRAYER**," "**FASTING**," and "**GOOD WORKS**" (for little children) or "**ALMSGIVING**" (for the older ones.)

- "**HOLY FAMILY**," with the reverse showing "**JESUS**," "**MARY**," and "**JOSEPH**."
- "**COMMUNION OF SAINTS**," with the reverse showing "**EARTH**," "**PURGATORY**," and "**HEAVEN**."
- "**CREED**," "**CODE**," and "**CULT**" (one on each leaf), with the reverse showing "**WHAT WE BELIEVE**," "**HOW WE BEHAVE**," and "**HOW WE WORSHIP**." This one would be used for the upper grades.

HOMILY

The homily should be quite obvious, given the five (less or more) shamrocks and what they indicate. You can be as simple or detailed in your explanations as you wish. If you are dealing with primary grades, you will probably eliminate the last shamrock listed above; but it plays quite well from the fourth grade up.

Remember that, while you will probably introduce the first shamrock by connecting it with some comments about St. Patrick, the shamrock is only a teaching device. So you might decide to focus on the Mass and make up a shamrock with "**LITURGY OF THE WORD**" on the front, while the reverse would show "**FIRST READING AND PSALM**," "**SEC-OND READING AND GOSPEL VERSE**," and "**GOSPEL AND HOM-ILY**."

A second shamrock could have "**LITURGY OF THE EUCHARIST**" on the front, while the reverse could show "**PRESENTATION OF GIFTS**," "**CONSECRATION**," and "**GREAT AMEN**."

A third shamrock could have "**COMMUNION RITE**" on the front, while on the reverse you could have "**LORD'S PRAYER**," "**LAMB OF GOD**," and "**HOLY COMMUNION**." These are just a few ideas as to how this shamrock device could be used to teach more than the Blessed Trinity.

25

The 'Begats'

(Birth of Mary, Christmas Eve)

There is no more difficult Gospel to preach to the assembly than that of Christmas Eve (Mt 1:1-25) or the Birth of Mary, September 8 (Mt 1:1-16, 18-23), which traces the genealogy of Jesus. While the newer translation has done away with what were known as "the begats," it is still a real test of pronunciation for the reader and patience for the listener. It was a layman, Dick Hilliard, who provided a very palatable solution to this dilemma, with a very imaginative use of four flash cards. The pronunciation of the names will still be something for the reader to work on, and the text still requires some explanation to the assembly, but at least the reading and hearing will hold their attention and thus prep them to be open to whatever comments and explanations you might offer in your homily.

I have used this device several times, and it never fails to get a favorable response from the people, along with their enthusiastic participation. I sense that they recognize the challenge this passage presents to both the reader and listener, and they are quite grateful that someone is making an effort to make it interesting — and even fun!

PROPS

Make four flash cards that are able to be seen at the back of the church. Mine are 12" x 24," and the words are printed in big block letters. If they are printed in different colors, they are all the more attractive. The first one has the word "**HUH?**" printed on it. The second has "**OH!**" The third has "**BOO!**" The fourth has "**CLAP!**" on one side and "**CHEER!**" on the other. "CHEER" can be multicolored if you wish, with sunburst rays around it.

On the back of the first three cards, write the word that is on the front in small print in the upper-right corner; this serves as a cue to what is on the front so that the four cards can be set facedown on the pulpit or lectern, and then you will know that you are holding up the correct one at the proper time. Of course, the one with "CLAP!" on the front has "CHEER!" on the back.

All that remains is to mark the text in the Lectionary so that you will know when to hold up the proper cards. You can also use small self-stick notes to mark the places in the text. If you do not wish to mark the text, I suggest that you photocopy it and then mark that copy, though I prefer to read from the Lectionary rather than from a piece of paper (the "disposable Word of God"!).

Below we have printed the "genealogy" portion of the Gospel (Mt 1:1-17), exactly as found in the Lectionary (for the Birth of Mary, use just Mt 1:1-16 for the genealogy section), with cues inserted. Try it a few times until you are comfortable, and then, when you get a chance, use it in the pulpit. I am confident you will be pleased with the result.

The book of the genealogy of Jesus Christ, the son of David, the son of Abraham.

Abraham became the father of Isaac,
    Isaac the father of Jacob,
    Jacob the father of Judah and his brothers. [CLAP!]
Judah became the father of Perez and Zerah,
    whose mother was Tamar. [BOO!]
Perez became the father of Hezron,
    Hezron the father of Ram,
    Ram the father of Amminadab. [HUH?]
Amminadab became the father of Nahshon,
    Nahshon the father of Salmon, [OH!]
    Salmon the father of Boaz,
    whose mother was Rahab. [BOO!]
Boaz became the father of Obed,
    whose mother was Ruth. [CLAP!]
Obed became the father of Jesse,
    Jesse the father of David the king. [CLAP!]

David became the father of Solomon,
    whose mother had been the wife of Uriah. [BOO!]
Solomon became the father of Rehoboam,

Rehoboam the father of Abijah,
Abijah the father of Asaph. [HUH?]
Asaph became the father of Jehoshaphat,
Jehoshaphat the father of Joram,
Joram the father of Uzziah. [OH!]

Uzziah became the father of Jotham,
Jotham the father of Ahaz,
Ahaz the father of Hezekiah.
Hezekiah became the father of Manasseh,
Manasseh the father of Amos,
Amos the father of Josiah. [HUH?]
Josiah became the father of Jechoniah and his brothers at the time of
the Babylonian exile. [OH!]

After the Babylonian exile, [BOO!]
Jechoniah became the father of Shealtiel,
Shealtiel the father of Zerubbabel.
Zerubbabel the father of Abiud.
Abiud became the father of Eliakim,
Eliakim the father of Azor, [HUH?]
Azor the father of Zadok.
Zadok became the father of Achim,
Achim the father of Eliud,
Eliud the father of Eleazar.
Eleazar became the father of Matthan,
Matthan the father of Jacob. [OH!]
Jacob the father of Joseph, the husband of Mary. [CLAP!]
Of her was born Jesus who is called the Christ. [CLAP!/CHEER!]

Thus the total number of generations
from Abraham to David,
is fourteen generations;
from David to the Babylonian exile,
fourteen generations;
from the Babylonian exile to the Christ,
fourteen generations.

26

Heart to Heart

(Sacred Heart, Jesus' Body and Blood)

The Mass for the closing of the school year fell on the feast of the Sacred Heart, so naturally we had to come up with a homily for all of the children on this wondrous sign of God's love for us. This turned out to be one of the simpler efforts — it took about 15 minutes to plan and about an hour to execute — and it actually brought applause from the youngsters! So here it is, and may you receive the same spontaneous affirmation from your students that I did.

PROPS

They are quite simple. You will need a piece of poster board that is white on one side and red on the other. You will also need a piece of foam core (white or blue) that is at least 24" x 30". You will need a dozen pushpins, a pair of scissors, and several erasable markers in bright colors.

Begin by drawing a heart in pencil on the white side of the poster board. Make it as large as you can within the confines of the usual 22" x 28" dimensions. Draw a red border on it so that it will be visible against the white or blue background. Now divide it into five sections, doing so with jagged lines so that they don't give away the figure of a heart before you put them together. (See illustration for suggested divisions.) Now cut out the five pieces.

On what will be the upper-left-hand section, print the word "**MERCY.**" On the upper-right-hand section, print the word "**BLOOD.**" On the left-middle section, print the word "**JOY.**" On the right-middle section, print the word "**PATIENCE.**" Finally, on the lower section, print the word "**LOVE.**" Each of these words should be printed in a different color.

Now turn all five pieces over, with the red side up, and reassemble the heart. Across the top two sections, print the word "**SACRED.**" Across the two middle sections, print the words "**HEART OF.**" On the bottom

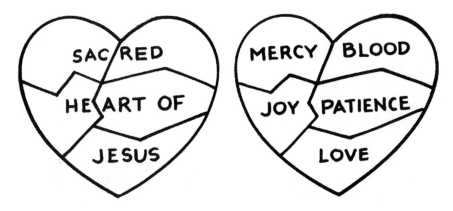

section, print the word "**JESUS**." (Don't do this piece by piece or it will come out wrong!)

Place the five pieces, with the white side up, on the foam core board and, using a *pencil*, draw the outline of the heart on the board. This will help you place the pieces correctly during the homily. Next, determine where you will put the pushpin in each piece so that the pieces will hang properly. You don't want them swinging out of position, thus destroying the heart figure.

Now turn the heart over, and arrange the red pieces in the same way. Put the pushpins in those pieces also so that they won't swing. Because of the irregular shapes of the pieces, the hole that holds each piece white-side-out will probably not be the same as the one to hold the piece with the red side out. If you wish, place a little pencil mark next to the holes on the red side so that you will know which ones they are — or you can use two pins.

Before you begin the homily, have the pieces lying flat on the altar or a small table, with a dozen pushpins next to them. (You will probably not use all of the pushpins, but it's good to have them handy. You may need two pins for some pieces.) Have the foam core board on an easel, or have one of the servers bring it forward and hold it.

HOMILY

Begin by stating that this is the feast of the Sacred Heart of Jesus (a term that the little ones may be hearing for the first time), and that you want to tell them some important things about this wonderful heart. Ask the children what a heart is and what it does. The older ones will tell you that it is a pump in the body that makes the blood flow through the whole body.

Now say that you found several scrap pieces of poster board in your closet, so you used them to make some signs. Hold up the piece marked "BLOOD," and speak about how important blood is to our body. Then tell how Jesus shed His blood for us on the cross and even gives us His Blood in Holy Communion. When you finish the comments on BLOOD, put the piece back on the altar. *Don't display it on the board at that time.* Also, be sure that when you are handling the piece, you don't let them see the red side.

Go on to the other pieces and speak about God's MERCY and for-giveness, His PATIENCE with us whenever we sin, the JOY He brings to us in His many graces and gifts, and the LOVE He showed for us when He died and rose. After you show each piece, put it on the altar or table. Again, be careful not to reveal the red side of the pieces.

Now tell them that you will stick them up on this (foam core) board to show them all together. Begin with the top left (MERCY), then the top right (BLOOD), next the middle left (JOY) and the middle right (PA-TIENCE), and finally the bottom piece (LOVE).

Review the message of each piece, and then say, "I wonder what would happen if we turned these over." To do this, because they are of irregular shapes, you can't simply turn them over in place. You will have to remove all five pieces and start to assemble them again. Do this as quickly as possible so that the red heart takes shape and they read the words SACRED HEART OF JESUS. (This is where they all applaud!) Ask the older ones to recall what word was on the other side of each piece (they will enjoy the challenge), and then relate each of those words once more to the Sacred Heart.

Two Final Suggestions.

1. When you are assembling the pieces the first time, you might choose not to put them up in the order suggested above but rather in a random order so that the image of the heart is not seen too soon. This bit of suspense holds their attention even more. To do this, however, you will have to draw an outline in pencil of each piece in

its proper location so that when you are finished, you have a good-looking heart!

2. When you speak of the word JOY, explain that the way to find real joy is to remember that in our daily lives we must put (J)esus first, (O)thers second, and (Y)ourself third. This little device can be very helpful, and it is easy to remember, both for you and for the children.

III

CHURCH TEACHINGS

27

Sin Enslaves Us, Jesus Saves Us

(Sin as Addiction, Firm Purpose of Amendment, Slaves Set Free)

This homily was developed for the campers to whom I minister in July. It is based on the Second Reading for the 13th Sunday of the Year (Year C), but I include it here because it can serve very well for *any* occasion on which you want to speak to children about the place of sin in their lives, how it can become a habit (we become a slave to it), and that the only way to get free of it is to turn to Jesus in the Sacrament of Reconciliation.

Moreover, after going to confession, they are to use the graces from that sacrament to continue to maintain the freedom from sin and growth in God's life (grace). You will find that this is perhaps a bit advanced for children who are preschool or in primary grades, where many of them hardly know what sin is; for them, it's mostly means being "naughty." But it challenges those in middle grades and even junior high to think about who they are (i.e., their own personal dignity, how sin distorts who they are, and how responding to God's grace leads them to real, genuine freedom).

As a matter of fact, when I speak to the middle-school grades about the wondrous gift of sex, I often use the first part of this presentation to help them understand what remarkable creations they are, how gifted they are in many different ways, and how the proper use of God's gift of sex and sexuality provides them with true freedom and an increase in self-esteem, something many teenagers lack or at least are confused about.

PROPS

You will need to make several signs. These should be on poster board pieces, 28" x 22". The pieces can each be a different color, or in the same color. But for the first two signs, use a different color for the printing of each line.

First Sign

This first sign will contain the following words:

WHAT MAKES ME A <u>PERSON</u>?
AN INTELLECT – <u>NOT</u> MY BRAIN. *(Note to the reader: The brain is the center of our nervous system, but not the facility that enables us to think.)*
- **I AM ABLE TO <u>THINK</u>.**
- **I AM ABLE TO <u>REMEMBER</u>.**
- **I AM ABLE TO <u>IMAGINE</u>.**

Second Sign

This sign will contain the following words:

WHAT ELSE MAKES ME A <u>PERSON</u>?
- **A FREE WILL.**
- **I MAKE CHOICES.**
- **I AM <u>RESPONSIBLE</u> FOR MY CHOICES.**
- **I DO NOT <u>BLAME</u> OTHERS.**

Third Sign

This sign will have the following words:

WHAT MAKES ME A <u>SLAVE</u>?
- **DISOBEYING**
- **LYING**
- **CHEATING**
- **CURSING**
- **FIGHTING**
- **BEING GREEDY**

Add or substitute other sins, depending on the age of the children you are addressing. These words should each be in a different color and can either be listed from top to bottom or printed at all different angles so as to catch the attention of those who see them.

All of these signs can either be made out of one piece of poster board and simply folded so as to show one panel at a time, or they can be made with the lines on separate pieces and hinged together with either transparent tape or masking tape. The idea is to reveal only one panel or section at a time. (Also see the instructions for the props in Chapter 4, "Martha and Mary," pages 44-45.)

An even simpler method would be to have all of the printing on one piece of poster board and simply use a blank piece that you can hold in front of the board, sliding it down to reveal one line at a time. The one drawback of this method is that you need an easel and have to stand next to it to hold that blank piece of poster board in its various positions, or have a child hold the poster board and the blank cover piece in place. You could also print the lines on foam core and fasten a blank piece of poster board over each line, fastening it with pushpins. Then just remove the pushpins and poster board to reveal each printed line.

Fourth Sign

This is optional, because the heart of the homily is in the first three signs listed above. However, this sign, plus a length of rope, will add a very visual and magical ending to the homily and clearly demonstrate what you are teaching. The sign should also be made of one piece of poster board, 28" x 22", but folded so that each half measures 14" x 22". The edges should be taped all around to form one double piece, thus making it more substantial. In the middle of this double piece cut a square hole 2"x 2". Finally, on one side print the words "**SINS MAKE US SLAVES!**" On the other side print "**JESUS SETS US FREE!**"

If you are going to use this fourth sign, you will also need a length of rope, about 8' to 10' long. It should be a soft rope, preferably white. (Cotton is preferable, but nylon is also usable.) You *apparently* are going to wrap this rope around the waist of a boy. (Don't use a girl for this unless the group is all girls!) The rope will represent how we can get bound up in sin. Then you will cause the rope *apparently* to pass through the boy's body, representing the freedom from sin that only Jesus can give.

PREPARATION: In addition to the rope, you will need two pieces of white Velcro (available at any fabric or hardware store.) Wrap each piece around the rope. When brought together, they stick until pulled apart.

PRESENTATION: After you have delivered the principal message using the signs as indicated above, select three boys from the group.

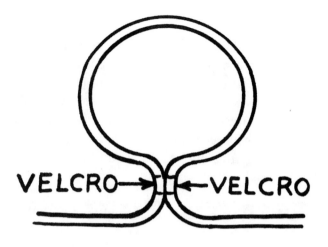

VELCRO→⊟←VELCRO

Have one of the boys stand in front of you. The other two should stand, one on each side of him, a couple of feet away from him. Hold up the sign with the square cutout, and show the group the side that says (and read this aloud) "SIN MAKES US SLAVES!" Now turn the other side around and let them see (and you read aloud) "JESUS SETS US FREE!" Give the sign to one of the other boys to hold.

Now show the rope, holding it outstretched between your hands, each hand covering a piece of the Velcro. (Because the Velcro bands are white and the rope is too, don't worry about them being seen should they slip from behind your fingers. Just move your hand to cover the band again. Remember, those watching know nothing about the Velcro.)

Pick up the rope and, holding the rope outstretched, lower it in front of the boy to his waist. Bring the rope around behind the boy (*saying that you will wrap it around his waist*) until your hands meet. Then connect the two pieces of Velcro and, instead of switching the ropes from hand to hand as you would if you were actually tying it around the boy's waist, bring the ends of the rope back around the sides of the boy on which you brought them to his back. (See illustration.)

Take the sign with the square hole in it, and turn it so the side that reads "JESUS SETS US FREE!" is facing the group. Give it to the boy in the middle, the one with the rope around him, to hold. Now feed the two ends of the rope through the hole, back to front. Ask the boys on the right and the left to each take an end of the rope and move to the side.

Then remind the group that the boy is tied up in sin. But Jesus saves us from sin

With that cue, tell the boys holding the ends of the rope to hold the end tight in their hand and then pull on it. The Velcro will separate and the entire rope will pass through the hole in the poster giving a perfect illusion that the rope has also passed through the boy's body and he is now free from sin! Emphasize this by taking the rope from the two boys and spreading it out between your hands. This also gives you the opportunity to cover the Velcro strips so they are not seen.

HOMILY

The theme of the homily is, of course, expressed in the first two signs. Begin, then, by holding up the first card that reads, "WHAT MAKES ME A PERSON?" The first point you want to make is that we are truly remarkable creatures, superior to all other animals. What makes us superior to them is our soul, which has the two great powers of intellect and will.

By using questions, do all you can to elicit these answers from the group. In short, try to get them *thinking*! Almost always, one of them will tell you we use the brain to think. Explain to them (as noted above) that the brain is the center of the nervous system. After all, all animals have brains, but they are not human. What is it that makes us distinctly human? The answer is the *intellect*. Reveal the second line of the sign.

Next, ask them what three things we do with the intellect. You will have to prompt them by questions to come up with "THINK," "REMEMBER," and "IMAGINE," but push them to *think*! You can ask what they think about and gradually lead them to conclude that they think with what they remember. Finally, have them look around and ask how all the things they see came to be, especially those things that humans have made. The answer is that someone had to imagine them — to *think* and *remember*, and then *imagine* something they wanted, how it should look, how it could be made, and so on. (This questioning process is not always easy, because so many of our youngsters we deal with do not do a whole lot of thinking. The media do it for them!)

Remember to reveal the appropriate lines of the signs as your homily progresses.

Now hold up the second sign that asks, "WHAT ELSE MAKES ME A PERSON?" The answer is "FREE WILL." Once you get that answer, ask them what it means. They will probably respond that we can do anything we want to do. For them, that is freedom. But we have to be RESPONSIBLE for our choices, and we therefore cannot BLAME anyone else for the outcome of what *we* choose to do. This is not an easy concept to get across because from their youngest days, children have learned to say, "He/She made me do it!" We have to teach them that, although other people can try to influence us in our decisions, we are the ones who make the final choice. (You might cite the example of the martyrs, who died before anyone could change their mind about their love for Jesus.)

Next, using the third sign, "WHAT MAKES ME A SLAVE?" introduce St. Paul's idea that when we misuse our freedom to choose, we become slaves of our sinful habits. "For example," you might say, "once we lie, we find it easier to lie the next time — but we also have to remember what we said so as to keep telling the same lie! We also usually lie because we have first disobeyed, and now we must lie to cover up our disobedience — so we become slaves to *two* sins!"

"Similarly," you can add, "the first time we curse or swear, we are somewhat surprised that it came out of our mouths; but it gets a bit easier each time we do it. Before long, we are using words that are wrong without even thinking about them. This does not makes us sound cool or tough; it makes us sound stupid because we cannot express ourselves in a proper way. We are slaves in speech to cursing and swearing." Continue with whatever other sins you have posted on the third sign.

The rest of the homily is yours to develop, but I *urge* you to spend time on the fact that we are responsible for the choices we make and we cannot blame others for those choices. I often tell the children that the word *blame* ought to be removed from the English language because it really is a cop-out, a denial of the fact that *we* are responsible for all that we say and do.

Once you have finished with the signs, then, if you wish, you can demonstrate the lesson in a way that the children will long remember by using the rope escape trick. Just don't present it as a trick. Rather, it is a way to demonstrate how sin makes us slaves, whereas Jesus sets us free!

28

The Good Shepherd

(God's Love, Forgiveness, Worth of Individual)

I cannot claim authorship of this idea. Credit goes to Dick Hilliard, a layman who gave a seminar on children's homilies which I attended, at which he presented this idea and the one for Chapter 25, "The 'Begats.' " I have used this presentation of the Good Shepherd parable several times and found it effective every time.

PROPS

All that are needed are ten pictures of the heads of sheep. (See illustration.). This image can be photocopied on white paper and then each picture mounted on green poster board, 10" x 13". You will also need a

good thick branch or pole to serve as the staff of the "shepherd." There is some rehearsal needed, which can be done in ten minutes. It involves an adult male to act as the shepherd and one young boy to act as the lost sheep. The rest is done on the spot.

Rehearsal

Tell the boy that you will count the "sheep" five times. When you do it the fifth time, and send the "sheep" out to play, he is to hide at a place you designate at the back of the church. When the "shepherd" comes in search of him, he is to make the typical sheep "baa" sound so that the "shepherd" can find him.

The "shepherd" is simply to count the "sheep" as you instruct him during the homily and then, when one is discovered missing, to go in search of him, at first going in a direction away from his (the sheep's) hiding place but ending up there to bring the lost sheep back to the fold.

HOMILY

Explain to the children that one of the most beautiful images of Jesus is that of the Good Shepherd. Ask them what a shepherd is. (If they are "city kids" and have not heard the Christmas story, they may not know.) Once this identity is established and you have introduced the gentleman who is to play the shepherd's role, then proceed to ask ten of the children to come forward to be his sheep. As each child does so, hand him/her a picture of a sheep. When they all are assembled across the front of the sanctuary, ask them what noise a sheep makes. They will all say, "Baa," and then you get on with the story.

"Once upon a time, there was a shepherd who took very good care of his sheep. Every morning before they went out into the fields, he would count his sheep. (*Ask the "shepherd" to do this aloud, counting from one to ten.*) Then he would send them out to play." (*At this point, tell the children to move about the sanctuary like sheep in the field, and they should be "baaing.*")

"Every night the shepherd would collect his sheep, and before letting them go to sleep, he would count them again to make sure they were all there. (*Have the "shepherd" count them, again out loud, from one to* ten.) The next day he did the same thing." (*Repeat the sequence. This time the children will feel a bit more "at home" in the sanctuary and probably wander farther, which is exactly what you want. If they don't do it, encourage them!*)

"One morning the shepherd counted his sheep (*have him do it*) and sent them out to play." (*Send the children out to do this. This time the boy that rehearsed the role should go down the side aisle to the designated spot and hide.*)

"That night he counted them again. (*This time the "shepherd" counts only nine and says aloud, "Nine." So you ask him:*) 'How many are you supposed to have?' (*He replies, "Ten." You say:*) 'Then count them again.' (*He counts them and again says, "Nine."*) And so, the good shepherd had to go out and find the lost sheep." (*At this point, the "shepherd" starts out into the church, heading away from the "sheep's" hiding place, and calling, "Little sheep, where are you?"*)

"Then he heard the cry of the lost sheep. (*The boy should be "baaing."*) He found him and carried him safely home. (*As you narrate this part of the story, embellishing it as you choose, the "shepherd" goes over to the hiding place, finds the "sheep," places him on his shoulder or in his arms, and carries him back to the rest of the sheep in the sanctuary.*) All the other sheep were very glad to see the lost sheep, and they all slept safely that night."

The acting out of this beautiful story can be very powerful. Don't be surprised if the children all applaud when the "shepherd" carries "home" the "lost sheep" (you might even cue them to do this) and some of the adults get teary-eyed. It is a beautiful moment and can make the love of God more visible than many pictures you have seen of the Good Shepherd.

29

'Take My Yoke Upon You'

(Jesus Always with Us, Encouragement in Difficulty, Failure, or Suffering)

Let me begin by confessing that I must have used the Gospel passage concerning the "Gentle Mastery of Christ" (see Mt 11:28-30; 14th Sunday of the Year, Cycle A) a couple hundred times without finding any real message in it. For years, I admired its poetic manner of expression but little more. As I'm from Manhattan's West Side in New York City, I found it difficult at first to relate to a yoke. Then I came across a commentary that opened my eyes and ears (and mind!) to its meaning, and it has become one of my favorite New Testament passages. I find it particularly powerful when anointing the sick or those preparing for surgery. It can also teach a very important and powerful lesson to the young.

PROPS

- **Yoke.** This can be made quite simply. (See illustration.) You will need two pieces of poster board (28" x 22"), a piece of wood 1" x 1" x 48", a 6' length of rope, and some Scotch tape.

  1. Fold the *two* pieces of poster board the long way – i.e., from top to bottom – but do not crease the fold.
  2. Tape the 22" ends together, and then the sides – up to about 6" from the fold.
  3. From each folded piece, cut a horseshoe-shaped piece about 8" wide and 9" high. Discard the U-shaped pieces, and then tape the edges of the U-shaped area.
  4. Slit the tape on the right side of one piece of poster board, and insert the other piece about 2" so they form a yoke. Now tape these together.

5. Insert the wood strip through the joined pieces so they are centered on the wood (i.e., with equal portions of the wood extending from the sides). Secure the joined pieces of poster board to the wood with thumbtacks or staples. Hammer a 1 1/2" nail into each end of the wood strip, and tie the rope ends on the strip between the end of the poster board and the nail. The purpose of the nail is to prevent the rope from slipping off the end of the wood strip. With a felt marker, write "**JESUS**" over one side of the yolk and "**ME**" on the other. Do this only on one side (see text of the homily). Keep the yoke out of sight until you are ready to show it.

- **Five Signs.** Three of the same color; two of a different color. On the first sign, print "**OBEY**" on one side and "**DISOBEY**" on the other; on the second sign, print "**TELL THE TRUTH**" on one side and "**TELL A LIE**" on the other; on the third sign, print "**SHARE WITH OTHERS**" on one side and "**BE SELFISH**" on the other. The fourth and fifth signs will be larger than the first three. On the fourth sign, print "**FEEL ALONE OR LEFT OUT?**" on one side and "**JESUS IS ALWAYS WITH YOU**" on the other. On the fifth sign, print "**SUFFER ALONE OR IN PAIN?**" on one side and "**JESUS IS YOUR STRENGTH**" on the other. You will need three children to assist. Finally, for this homily to be successful, it should be rehearsed!

HOMILY

You might start out by saying, "This Gospel passage sounds very beautiful, even poetic, but what does it mean? Let's begin by talking about what a yoke is. A yoke is a large piece of wood used to hold two animals together. It is used most often with two oxen, sometimes two horses, to pull a plow, a heavy load, or turn a millstone. *(You might want to explain the millstone.)* One of the animals is usually stronger than the other, and it is trained to be the lead animal. That means it is trained to go where the farmer directs it. Because the two animals are bound together by the yoke, the other animal follows the lead animal wherever it goes. Together they do the work that has to be done.

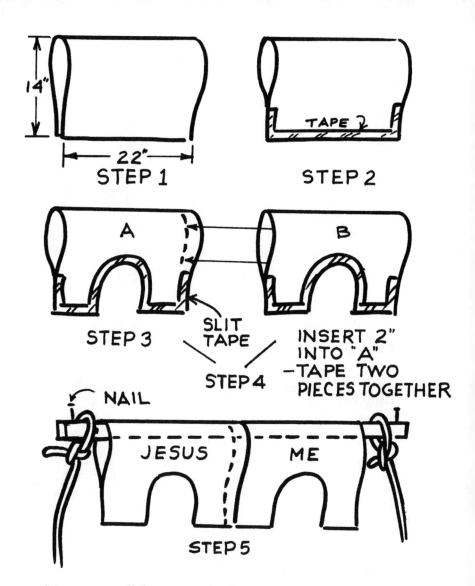

14"

22"

STEP 1

TAPE

STEP 2

A

B

STEP 3

SLIT
TAPE

STEP 4

INSERT 2"
INTO "A"
—TAPE TWO
PIECES TOGETHER

NAIL

JESUS   ME

STEP 5

"You may recall that Jesus was the town carpenter, and so He made the yokes for the farmers in His town. He knew they were custom-made to fit the very animal that would wear it. They were not 'one size fits all'! You know how it hurts when your feet grow and your shoes are too small. You need to buy new shoes that are comfortable. So the yokes were made to fit each animal comfortably. As a result, whenever the animal grew larger, a new yoke was made that fit comfortably. The reason was to reduce the chafing and rubbing on the shoulders of the animal so that it would make it as easy as possible to pull the plow or the heavy load. Jesus refers to all of this in this Gospel passage.

"Now let's look at a yoke. (*Bring it into view.*) Here are the two places for the necks of the animals, and this rope is for the farmer to steer them. How does this fit into the Gospel?

"The key sentence is Jesus saying, 'Take *my* yoke upon you and learn from *me*, for I am meek and humble of heart.' The emphasis is on the word *my*. Jesus is saying it is *His* yoke, and He asks us to share it with Him. (*Turn the yoke around to reveal the words JESUS and ME.*) So Jesus is here. (*Point to one opening.*) And you and I, if we so choose, are over here. (*Point to the other opening.*) Who do you think is holding the rope and steering? God the Father! He reveals His will to Jesus, who always does His Father's will. So Jesus will always lead you in the right direction. Now let's see how it works."

(*At this point, one of the three youngsters (#1) will move into the JESUS slot, another (#2) into the ME slot, and the third (#3) will prepare to hand you the signs. You take the reins, and #1 and #2 are "in" the yoke.*)

"Suppose your mother, teacher, or coach asks you to do something but you don't want to. (*#3 holds up the DISOBEY sign and hands it to #2.*) Now you want to disobey, but Jesus tells you to obey. (*As this is said, #2 hands the sign to #1, who flips it to show OBEY.*) You may still want to disobey, and unlike the ox that is locked in the yolk, you can walk away and disobey! (*Have #2 walk out of the yolk.*) But if you choose to let Jesus lead you on the right way, you will walk with Him and find peace." (*#2 moves back into the yoke. #1 drops the sign to the floor or hands it back to #3, who goes to #1 to retrieve it.*)

"Suppose you disobey and get caught — as usually happens. Now you want to lie your way out of it. (*#3 shows the TELL A LIE sign and hands it to #2.*) This often happens: We disobey, and then we lie. Again, Jesus says it is the Father's will to tell the truth. (*#2 hands the sign to #1, who flips it over to show TELL THE TRUTH.*) Again, you can walk away (*#2 does so*) or walk with Jesus. (*#2 returns to the yoke.*) Jesus wants us to do the Father's will."

(*Use the card BE SELFISH/SHARE WITH OTHERS, as you did the previous two cards.*)

"But Jesus is not at our side just to keep us from sinning. He is always there to support and comfort us. For example, suppose we feel lonely. Perhaps we're the new kid on the block, or in the school, or at camp, or on a team." (*#3 gives you the sign FEEL ALONE OR LEFT OUT? and you show it to the children.*)

"Perhaps we are an only child with no one to play with, or suppose a group we would like to belong to won't let us in. Then it is very important to remember that (*flip the sign*) JESUS IS <u>ALWAYS</u> WITH YOU! He is the one Friend who is always by your side to support you and tell you that He loves you.

"Or suppose you are hurt, in pain, or very upset. (*Show the sign SUFFERING ALONE OR IN PAIN?*) Maybe you are sick or have failed at something important to you. Maybe your parents are fighting with each other, or you have been embarrassed or humiliated by someone. Then it is very important to remember that (*flip the sign*) <u>JESUS</u> IS YOUR STRENGTH."

Comment on these last two posters. Then review the whole presentation, and bring the homily to a conclusion.

30

The Devil Bopper!

(Power of God's Grace, Fighting Temptation, Prayer, Devil)

The title is a clear indication of what this homily is about: Bopping the Devil! It also describes what may be the children's homily from which I got the greatest children's response. The homily itself was a response to a difficult selection from the Gospel reading (see Mk 1:29-39; Fifth Sunday of the Year, Cycle B) that told of Jesus healing someone (Peter's mother-in-law), going off to pray alone, and then driving Devils out of those who were possessed. I was faced with three difficult and challenging topics: (1) healing (for most children this means a kiss on the boo-boo and the application of a multicolored Band-Aid), (2) going off to pray alone (many of the youngsters I was addressing knew no prayers at all, other than those they "said" with the family), and (3) dealing with the Devil. I chose to deal with the Devil. I prayed each day for four days for some idea as to how to bring this very serious and important message to children, but kept coming up with nothing. Suddenly, on the Thursday before I was to give the homily, while I was praying in our chapel, the idea came to me: Bop the Devil! So I set out to collect the necessary props.

PROPS

- A "Devil Bopper." At first, I searched for a foam-rubber baseball bat, but I couldn't find any in the stores. A whiffle bat was too hard for my purpose (it would hurt the person to be "bopped"). At a local toy store, I asked a clerk if he had anything with which I could hit someone but without hurting him/her. (In this era of child abuse, that was a risky question!) He looked at me with a whole series of questions running through his head, none of which he asked, thank goodness, and then suggested that at the end of one of the aisles I might find a jousting stick — the kind used on the TV show "American Gladiators." I looked, discovered it was just what I needed, and bought the only one they had left. The jousting stick is a plastic tube about 24" long, with a large foam-rubber ball fastened on each end. (With that description, you can probably make one if you can't buy one.) This should be hidden until ready to be shown to the children.

- Four sleeves made of construction paper, each of which can slip over one end of the stick and on each of which is printed one of the following words: "**OBEY**," "**SHARE**," "**TRUTH**," and "**PRAY**." The word should appear on both sides of the sleeve so that no matter what side is facing the child, the word can be read.
- A tray on which these four sleeves are placed.
- A separate sleeve on which "**GRACE**" is printed on one side and "**POWER**" on the other.
- A piece of red material (cotton is cheap and works fine) on which are fastened two pieces of Velcro. These should be on adjacent corners so that the cloth can be fastened and work like a cape.
- A black or red mask that covers the eyes of the "Devil."
- A large plastic pitchfork. These are available in costume or toy stores, especially around Halloween.

(Special Note: For this homily, you will have to enlist the assistance of a boy at least ten years old. He is to play the Devil. I was able to get a specific youngster about 15 minutes before Mass to play the part after a very brief rehearsal, but you might want to be better prepared than that and have someone rehearsed the day before. Your assistant will wear the cape and mask and carry the pitchfork. He should remain out of sight until you introduce him.)

HOMILY

I began the homily by explaining to the parents the quandary I experienced while trying to prepare for this homily. I did this as the children were coming from their seats, so they weren't paying attention to the remarks (those found in the first paragraph of this homily presentation). It was also to allay their fears that I was about to frighten their children by speaking to them about the Devil. Some parents just want to pretend that their children never do anything wrong, or at least are not tempted by anyone other than a sibling!

Once the children were gathered, I began to speak to them about the Devil. I told them the Devil was once a good angel but had turned against God and disobeyed Him.

"Ever since that time, the Devil has not been allowed into heaven. And since he is unhappy about that, he tries to get other people to do bad things so they can be unhappy with him.

"However, God gives us special help to fight against the Devil. That special help is a gift called *grace* and it allows us to *bop the Devil* whenever he tries to get us to do something wrong. Let me show you my Devil Bopper."

Here you take it out for the first time. (I had placed mine on the floor behind the altar since I don't stand there until the Preparation of the Gifts.) The sleeve with the words GRACE and POWER on it should be fixed permanently on one end of the Bopper. An altar server should now bring over the tray on which are the other sleeves.

Tell the children that grace is God's special power — turn the Bopper so that they can see both sides and, therefore, both words. Have them repeat the phrase "Grace is power!" as you show them the two sides alternately. Tell them God gives us this power so we can bop the Devil when he tries to get us to commit a sin.

At this point, you tell them that someone has volunteered to play the part of the Devil. Introduce him, but don't tell his name (you'll do that at the end of the homily), and have him stand off to the side a bit so that they can see him while you present the three choices about which they will choose to bop the Devil.

Now give them four examples. You may choose mine or make up your own.

"First, your mom tells you that she is expecting company and asks you to clean up your room before they come. You are watching TV so you say, 'Okay, Mom,' but go on watching the TV. Then God speaks to you in your heart and says, 'I want you to obey your mom,' and He gives you the grace to do that." (*At this point, slip the sleeve with the word OBEY on the other end of the Bopper, the one without a sleeve. I suggest that you place the tray on the altar and have the server hold the Bopper while you slip the sleeve on the proper end.*)

"What does God tell us to do? (*The children will say, "Obey."*) But what does the Devil tell us to do? (*The boy playing the Devil should say, in his most "devilish" voice, "Disobey, kids, disobey!"*) But what does God tell us to do with His power to obey? (*Point to the GRACE sleeve.*) 'Bop the Devil!' "(*With this, invite one of the children to take the Bopper in hand and bop the Devil on the head. When the child does this, the "Devil" should stagger around, but not fall. This will get a wonderful reaction from the* grown-ups as well as the children. As noted, if these homilies are delivered with enthusiasm, the entire assembly will get involved and learn from them!)

"After the visitors are gone, your mom says that there are cookies left over, and that you should keep them until the next day and share them with your brother, sister, or friend. God says in your heart, 'Share the cookies,' but the Devil says, 'Be greedy, kids, be greedy!' What does God say? (The kids will call out, "Share the cookies!") But what does the Devil say? (The "Devil" should say, "Be greedy, kids, be greedy!") So what do we do? All together: Bop the Devil!" (As you are going through this part, remove the OBEY sleeve and slip the SHARE sleeve on the Bopper. Then have a child come up and bop the Devil. The "Devil" should stagger a bit more this time.)

"The next day your mother asks you if you shared the cookies. Let's suppose you didn't. God says in your heart, 'Tell the truth.' (Here slip on the TRUTH sleeve.) But the Devil says, 'Lie, kids, lie, or you'll get in even more trouble!' But God says we should tell the truth, so what should we do to the Devil?" (All cry out, "Bop the Devil!" Another child gets to bop the Devil, and he really staggers around but does not fall.)

"There are many other things the Devil can try to get us to do, like be mean to our friends, talk back to our parents, or tease our brothers and sisters. The best thing we can do every day to use God's power *not* to do these things is to *pray*. Yes, prayer is the most powerful weapon we have to fight against the Devil. So what does God tell us in our hearts we should do when the Devil tries to get us to do bad things? He tells us to pray. What does He tell us to do?" (They will all shout, "PRAY!" Again, remove the SHARE sleeve and slip on the PRAY sleeve. With this, have another child come up and bop the Devil three times. The "Devil" should stagger around and then fall flat on his back (being careful, of course!) onto the floor. This may well bring a round of cheers and applause!)

"And that's how God wants us to be good. We are to bop the Devil!"

"So remember, boys and girls, that we have God's power, which we call *grace*. And when we use it, we can always bop the Devil and always be good."

Be sure to have the young fellow who plays the Devil stand up at the end, remove his mask, and take a bow. Thank him for doing so well. Have the children applaud, remarking that this isn't the real Devil but just someone playing the part of the Devil. This helps remove any fear about the masked person and will also give the young fellow a chance to feel better about himself after having played the enemy!

31

The Ten Gifts of the Holy Spirit

(Holy Spirit Active in Our Lives, Multipurpose Teaching Device)

Yes, I know that we all learned that the gifts of the Holy Spirit are seven, but that didn't fit into my plan for this homily — so now there are ten! Besides, have you ever tried to explain to a group of children, ages ten and under, the difference between wisdom, counsel, knowledge, and understanding? I'm not sure I could do that with a group of *adults*. So when I was challenged to compose a new homily for the Family Mass on Pentecost Sunday (there is another one for Pentecost, in Chapter 22, "The Spirit in the Wind"), I worked out a plan that focused on the Holy Spirit while listing ten gifts that He gives us (there could have been many, many more). The reason for the ten is that there are ten letters in the words *Holy Spirit*. So much for justification. Now on to the props!

PROPS

You will need 1 or 2 books of construction paper (preferably the 18" x 12" size); a pair of scissors; a glue stick; 2 pieces of foam core (red if you can get it), one 24" x 9", the other 36" x 9"; 20 pushpins, either clear or red; 10 jumbo paper clips; and Scotch tape. You will also need a set of 52 letters — actually 17 different letters in different quantities — and these can be obtained in one of the two ways indicated below. (See "B" below.)

A. Begin by measuring out and cutting 62 background pieces (i.e., pieces on which you will paste the letters). Select 10 different colored sheets from the construction paper book. Measure these off so that you get pieces 6" x 6" (easily done if you use the 18" x 12" sheets). Cut out 10 of these in *red* for the 10 letters in **HOLY SPIRIT**. Then cut out as many pieces as you will need to have one for each remaining letter. If possible, the color of the background pieces should be different for each word, while the background pieces for each letter in a specific word should be the same. Since children read horizontally, and these words are to be read vertically, the different color background for each word will enable the children to distinguish each word from the one(s) next to it. For example, the background pieces for the word HOLY could be blue (except, of course, for the first letter, H, which is on a red piece, as are all the letters of the words HOLY SPIRIT). The letters O, L, and Y could be yellow, giving you yellow letters on a blue background.

B. Now here are those two ways to make the letters:
   1. Go to the local art shop or office-supply store and ask for stencils for the letters. They come in several sizes including 5". Use these to make your letter, tracing them on different colored paper, then cutting them out, and pasting them on the background piece. This also allows you to make the letters of each word a different color (e.g., the letters for the word HOLY could be yellow on a blue background; for the word OBEY, they could be pink on a yellow background; and for the word OBEY, they could be blue with a pink background. Work at achieving good visibility by providing a clear contrast between the background piece and the letter.
   2. Go to the same local art shop or office-supply store and ask for vinyl letters. They are stick-ons and come in various sizes, but only in two or three colors (black, white, and perhaps red). They are easier and faster to use, but they lack the variety of colors obtainable when you provide the color.

C. Once the square background pieces have been cut and the letters mounted on them, it is time to assemble the whole production. First, attach the background pieces of each word by taping them in the proper order so they hinge and fall one below the other. Now accordion-fold upward the panels for each word so that they all sit on the first square (the red one bearing one of the letters of HOLY SPIRIT). If there is a blank space facing you, then a number can be printed on it. (This will be those words with an even number of letters, those starting with H, O, L, or P.) The other six words (with an odd number of letters) will have a letter facing you, so refold the letters so that the number is printed *inside* the next-to-last panel. This will produce a blank space on which you can print a large number. (See illustration.)

D. The final step is to arrange these letters on the foam core. (I found this worked better and the first letter lasted longer if I first mounted each of the first letters [HOLY SPIRIT] on a piece of poster board. It

Setup - Odd Number of Panels

Number goes here—
Second-to-last Panel

Setup - Even Number of Panels

Number goes on
Last Panel

provided a substantial backing. Any color will do since it won't be seen.) This is done with the pushpins.

1. On the 24" x 9" board of foam core, attach the words that begin with the letters H-O-L-Y: (1) HEAVEN, (2) OBEY, (3) LOVE, and (4) YES. Use the pushpins. The pins will go through the board and stick out on the reverse side. The board is 9" deep, so the altar servers holding them can do so on the side at the bottom 3 inches. Holding them there also assures that they don't knock any of the sets of letters off before or during the homily! Now mount the remaining six sets of letters on the 36" x 9" board, those words beginning with the letters S-P-I-R-I-T: (5) SHARE, (6) PRAY, (7) IMITATE, (8) RESPECT, (9) INSPIRE, and (10) THANK.

2. When they are all pinned on, then slip one of the jumbo paper clips at the top of each set of letters so they don't unfold ahead of time. (Only the number of the word should be showing at this point.) During the homily, as each number is called out by the children, simply remove the clip and the panels will open and fall down, revealing the letters which spell the gift. (See illustration.)

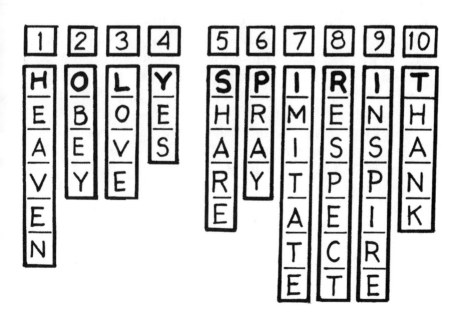

3. Finally, it will take a couple of hours to do all the above, which calls for two comments. First, this is a wonderful time to get other people involved! If you have a Children's Liturgy Committee, have the members make all of those panels and letters. Or get some older children to help. Either way, those who do help will be delighted to see their work *unfold* as you pull the clip on each word. The other reason why the investment of time is worth it is that this homily can be used for older children as well, right through high school, either at a liturgy or on a school retreat. The nature of the contents of the homily is such that it can be applied to any age group.

HOMILY

The content of the homily was really quite simple once the idea of the ten gifts was formed. I wanted the children (and their parents) to come to a deeper understanding of how the Holy Spirit gives us all the gifts we need to be good Catholics. So I took the ten letters that form the words HOLY SPIRIT and reflected on what gifts could be listed, each one beginning with one of the letters in those two words. Moreover, the gifts would be things the Holy Spirit helps us to accomplish so that we do what God our Father wants us to do. I talked about how Jesus came to make God visible, and now He calls us to follow His example so that we can make Jesus visible to others by what we say and do in our lives. To help us do that, He sends His Holy Spirit, who gifts us with grace, the power of being able to do the Father's will, especially when it's hard, when we really don't want to.

Once you have set the scene, produce the two foam core boards bearing the ten gifts. These are numbered 1 through 10. One of the children is asked to call off one of the numbers. You remove the paper clip, allowing the attached panels to fall open spelling out one of the gifts. As each is selected and revealed, you make a few simple comments on it, and then move on. Wherever possible, show how they relate to one another. For example, how YES relates to OBEY, and how both relate to LOVE; or how PRAY relates to THANK (Eucharist!) and how they both relate to the gifts.

At the end, you ask them who gives them all of these wonderful gifts that help us become holy people. Many of the older ones will have already spotted the ten cards across the top, which spell out "HOLY SPIRIT." Develop that thought, review the gifts the Spirit gives, perhaps have them join with you in a brief prayer of thanksgiving for the gifts, and then send them back to their seats.

Somewhere during this time, be sure to call the *adults'* attention to the gifts, stressing that they, too, have received them, and perhaps asking those who have been confirmed whether they have allowed these gifts — and all the others they have received — to have a real effect in their lives. (Don't ever ignore the parents and other adults present by preaching only to the children. Your homily should carry a message to the grown-ups, too.)

Those ideas produced this list of things the Holy Spirit helps us to do or achieve: H = Heaven, O = Obey, L = Love, Y = Yes, S = Share, P = Pray, I = Imitate, R = Respect, I = Inspire, and T = Thank. You could use other gifts according to your liking, but each should begin with one of the letters in the two words HOLY SPIRIT. Unless, of course, you choose to use the word PENTECOST! Then you will have to think up your own gifts!

32

The Rich Man and Lazarus

(Heaven and Hell, Sharing, Depth of God's Mercy)

This was another somewhat difficult part of the Gospel (see Lk 16:19-31; 26th Sunday of the Year, Cycle C) to relate to children. It spoke of hell and the eternal separation that results from being condemned to an eternal punishment. However, two things worked in my favor. First, while preparing a homily for the adults that weekend, I came across (was led to?) an old Russian folktale that suited my purposes quite well. All I had to do was adapt it to our culture. The second favorable circumstance was that it was Halloween season, and the party shops were filled with costumes. So off I went to one of those shops, where I purchased children's costumes for an angel and a witch (or an old woman). (Actually, I was to learn later that a number of the small children already had these costumes, so I could have borrowed them instead of purchasing them. It helps to check the children's "inventory" on occasions such as this; you might save some money.)

PROPS

1. Having reworked the story as you will read it below, I needed to find some kind of token for the Angel to offer to the Old Woman. The legend uses an onion offered to a peasant. I wasn't sure the children would know what an onion was, nor could I find a way to have it break in half as the story required. Instead, I bought a bag of candy and poured half of it into a zip-lock plastic bag, sealing the bag. Then I placed this into a second bag without sealing it. This would be given to the Angel at the proper time. Have it in your pocket ready to give to the angel at the proper time. The remainder of the candy should go into another bag to be presented to the Old Woman when the play is over. This can be in your other trouser pocket.

2. As noted above, you will need two costumes, one for the Old Woman (witch), and the other for the Angel.

3. The entire text of the folktale can be printed in large type on two pages, which are then pasted on pieces of poster board. These are for your use, and the poster board will make them stiff and easy to hold. Similar scripts, for the parts of the Angel and the Old Woman, can also be prepared this way and given to the two girls who will play the parts. A fourth copy of the script should be prepared for the Voice of God (see Prop #4). There is nothing to memorize; all will read as if telling a story.

4. To add a delightfully theatrical note, it will really intrigue the children if they can hear the "Voice of God" as "He" speaks to the angel! This is simply arranged. Enlist the help of a man with a deep voice, perhaps one of your good lectors, and give him the fourth copy of the script. He should also be given a microphone and asked to go into a room out of sight. He should be able to hear you over the church sound system and speak his parts over the microphone. The effect is wonderful and will have the children listening very attentively while looking around for the source of the voice. This same effect can be obtained by having a headset plugged into the amplifier and worn by the one providing the Voice of God so that he can hear the story and speak his lines into his microphone, even if he is in a space somewhat removed from earshot.

With the gimmicked bag of candy in one of your pockets, the prize bag in the other, and the children dressed in their costumes but out of sight, you are ready to begin.

HOMILY

Tell the children that they are going to hear an exciting story that originally came from Russia. It is also going to teach us all a very important lesson. Then read the story as follows (you are the Narrator):

Narrator: Once upon a time, there was a very wicked old lady. (*Here the Old Woman makes her entrance.*)

Narrator: She complained about everything.

Old Woman: (in a mean, cackling voice) Yesterday it was too hot, and today it is too cold.

Narrator: She was mean to everyone.

Old Woman: You wretched little children! Get out of my yard! I told you that you can't play there!

Narrator: She also was very selfish.

Old Woman: If you want what I have, go get some yourself!

Narrator: And nobody liked her at all. Now when she had finished her time on earth, she died, just as everyone does. Jesus has told us that dying is not a bad thing. It simply means that our life on earth is over, and if we have been really good, we will go to heaven to be with God and all the saints and all the other good people forever and ever. So the wicked Old Woman was taken up to stand before God, to find out where she would be forever — in heaven, with all the good people, or in hell, with all the bad people. Because she had been such a terrible person while she was on earth, God had no choice but to send her to hell, so He said to her:

Voice of God: Because you have been so bad, I have to send you to hell to be with the Devil and all the other wicked and mean and spiteful and selfish people who have ever lived.

Narrator: Now just like all of us, even though the wicked Old Woman was such a bad person, she had a Guardian Angel to watch over her all the time she was alive on earth. (*Here the Angel makes her entrance.*) The Guardian Angel tried very hard to get the wicked Old Woman to be good, but she had had no success. The Guardian Angel was very sorry that the wicked Old Woman ended up in hell, so she tried to think if there was even one little good deed that the woman had done. She thought, and she thought, and she thought. She was trying to think of even one good thing she could tell God about. Suddenly, she remembered something! So she went to God and said:

Angel: Dear God, I remember one day, a long time ago, that the wicked Old Woman had stolen a bag of candy. But on her way home, she saw a little child crying because he was hungry. Much to my surprise, the wicked Old Woman gave the candy to the little boy!

Narrator: And God said:

Voice of God: Are you sure of that, my dear angel?

Narrator: And the Angel said:

Angel: Oh, yes, I am quite sure. I remember it well because it was the only kind thing I ever saw her do!

Narrator: Then God said:

Voice of God: I will give you a bag of candy like the one the wicked Old Woman gave to that little boy. (*As these words are spoken, take the gimmicked bag – i.e., the bag-within-a-bag – out of your pocket and give it to the Angel.*) Let the wicked Old Woman take hold of it, and see if you can pull her out of hell with it. If she holds on to it and you can pull her out, then she can come to heaven. But if she lets go or does anything wrong, then she must stay where she is.

Narrator: So the Angel went down to the wicked Old Woman and said:

Angel: Take hold of the bag of candy, and I will pull you out of hell.

Narrator: The wicked Old Woman grabbed on to the bag of candy, and the angel began very slowly to pull her out of hell. (*The Angel and the Old Woman do what you are describing.*) But when the other bad people saw that she was being pulled out of hell in the direction of heaven, they began to grab on to her so that they could be pulled up to heaven, too! (*Coach a few of the children who are nearby to do this.*) Then the wicked Old Woman began to push them away (*the Old Woman pushes away those who are trying to grab at her clothes*), and she cried out:

Old Woman: I'm the one to be pulled out, not you. The bag of candy is mine, not yours. Get away from me. The candy is all mine! (*When these words are spoken, the Angel releases the outside bag, leaving it in the hands of the Old Woman, who is now holding an empty bag. The Angel continues to hold the bag filled with candy.*)

Narrator: As soon as the Old Woman said that, she found herself holding an empty bag – and the Angel had all the candy. The wicked Old Woman went back down into hell, to stay there forever. *(The Old Woman falls to the floor, still reaching out for the bag)* The Guardian Angel went away sad, because the wicked Old Woman had not changed. *(The Angel walks off with her head bowed in sorrow for the Old Woman.)* Even when God gave the Old Woman a special chance to get out of hell, she was still very selfish and would not share the candy with others. So God had no choice but to leave her there. So, boys and girls, the lesson of the story is *not* that there is anything wrong with having nice things, like a bag of candy, but that it is wrong if we are selfish and don't share what we have with others.

You may want to add further comments to bring the homily to a conclusion. Then, before you send the children back to their seats, be sure to thank the two girls who played the roles, and take the second bag of candy from your pocket and give it to the girl who played the Old Woman as a sign of your gratitude to her for playing the role. (The girl playing the Angel already has a bag in her hand.)

The only thing you have to teach the girls playing the Angel and the Old Woman before you begin is how to hold the full bag and the empty one around it so that, when the Old Woman makes her selfish statement, she will pull away the empty bag and leave the candy-filled one in the hand of the Angel.

Obviously, this homily will take some preparation, but the time will be well invested. There is no story to learn (photocopy the script that is here, if you wish), and just do a read-through with the two girls and the man playing the Voice of God beforehand. It would add a lot if the Old Woman and the Angel memorized their parts so they did not need the script, but this is not necessary. The lesson is important, the story is strong, and the introduction of other characters than yourself – plus the Voice of God! – will surely hold the attention of the children.

33

Excuses! Excuses!

(Growth, Responsibility, Self-esteem, Developing One's Own Gifts)

One of the most important lessons we can teach our youths is that they must be ready at all times to accept responsibility for everything they do. We live at a time when society offers us all sorts of opportunities to deny responsibility for our actions – no-fault divorce, no-fault insurance, and no-fault sex (that's what abortion is all about). It has also become very fashionable to blame our present actions on the impact our family has made on us, so much so that it seems that if we *don't* come from a "dysfunctional family," there must be something wrong with us!

This homily deals with that enormous problem of accepting personal responsibility and was written in response to the Gospel in which three different people offer excuses to Jesus as to why they cannot follow Him right then (see Lk 9:51-62; 13th Sunday of the Year, Cycle C). As you will see, it can be used for young people of all ages, and it would be quite applicable even at a teen retreat, a day of reflection, or a vocations talk.

PROPS

Four poster boards, 22" x 28", with printing on both sides. I suggest that the printing be such that the boards can be flipped over instead of turned around. Also, this is one time when it would be good to have the four persons holding the boards stand up front from the beginning. This holds the interest of the listeners to see what's coming next. The signs read as follows:

1. "**BE <u>ALL</u> THAT <u>YOU</u> CAN BE!**" with the reverse side showing "**DO THE VERY <u>BEST</u> THAT <u>YOU</u> CAN DO!**"
2. "**<u>HE/SHE</u> MADE ME DO IT!**" with the reverse side showing "**DON'T BLAME OTHERS!**"

3. **"I FORGOT!"** with the reverse side showing "**JUST DO IT — EVEN IF YOU DON'T LIKE IT!**"
4. **"I DIDN'T UNDERSTAND!"** with the reverse side showing "**ASK QUESTIONS!**"

HOMILY

Begin by calling attention to the three characters in the Gospel. Two of them offered to follow Jesus, and one of them was actually invited by Jesus to be one of His followers. However, all three offered excuses why they couldn't follow Him right then. Jesus makes the point that once we decide to follow Him, we must reject anything that gets in the way of our fulfilling that generous response. He will accept no excuses.

In effect, Jesus is saying, "BE ALL THAT <u>YOU</u> CAN BE!" Show the first sign. Ask the listeners where they have heard this slogan; they will undoubtedly say, "The U.S. Army commercial." To more clearly show what this means, have the first youngster flip the card and read, "DO THE VERY <u>BEST</u> THAT <u>YOU</u> CAN DO!" Here stress the need for us *not* to compare ourselves with others or to enter into competition with others, but rather strive to be the very *best* that *we* can be.

This idea actually can relieve a great deal of the pressure that young people (and some adults!) put on themselves to be like someone else who may be more talented, more gifted, older, smarter, etc., than they, but who also does not possess that unique combination of gifts and talents that they themselves have. All God asks of us is to do the best that *we* can do with what He gives us. If He expects no more from us, then why do we expect more of ourselves? This addresses a very common problem that leads to young people having an undeserved poor image of themselves. This, I feel, is one reason why they think God could never be calling them to His service.

Now introduce three excuses we frequently make for not being all *we* can be. The First Excuse is "<u>HE/SHE</u> MADE ME DO IT!" This is the ultimate cop-out that we all too often learn in earliest childhood. For example, "Why did you hit your little brother/sister?" We respond, "He/she made me do it because he/she hit me first." Here you must point out and emphasize how untrue this is. We respond to the actions of another with our own actions, but *we make the choice of how we respond.* There is nothing we do that we do not choose to do. Provide several examples of this. Then have the sign flipped over to show "DON'T BLAME OTH-ERS!" I have often said that we need to eliminate the word *blame* from the English language because almost always it is used to put the responsibility for our own actions onto someone else. This placing of blame is both unfair and untrue.

We are responsible (i.e., "able to respond") for our actions. (You might think of taking a felt-tip marker and drawing a line right through the word BLAME.)

The Second Excuse is "I FORGOT!" Cite examples of this: "I didn't do my homework . . . I didn't hang up my clothes . . . I didn't clean my room . . . I didn't take out the garbage . . . because *I forgot!*" To emphasize the point, I use the "example" of Jesus praying in the garden. But then, before the soldiers can come and arrest Him, He goes for a walk outside the city. God the Father asks, "But I thought You were going to go through the Passion for all sinners." And Jesus answers, "I forgot!" This may sound silly, but the kids react and see how feeble a response this is. Flip the sign over to show that it reads, "JUST DO IT – EVEN IF YOU DON'T LIKE IT!" This is really what is behind the excuse, "I forgot." We really don't want to do what we are asked or are supposed to do. Here you can briefly discuss the need we have to complete our assignments, do our chores, finish unpleasant tasks, etc., because once they're done, we can get back to what we want to do.

I often insert here the idea that there is no such thing as a mother who is born a nag. We children *make* them nags by not doing what we are supposed to do right away! If we did what we are asked, our mothers, fathers, teachers, coaches, etc., would never have anything to nag us about! (This goes over very well with the moms who are present!)

The Third Excuse – "I DIDN'T UNDERSTAND!" – really means either I didn't care enough to ask questions or I was too embarrassed to do so. Have the board flipped over to show "ASK QUESTIONS!" Then you might cite the example of a good teacher who says to the class, "Either you ask questions and you learn free of charge, or I ask the questions and it can cost you points on a test!" It is also appropriate here to speak of *negative peer pressure* (which, out of concern for what others might think, keeps one from asking questions that will help one to learn) and *positive peer pressure* (which enables one not only to get the information one needs but also sets a good example for those who are afraid to do so). Asking questions shows intelligence, not the lack of it.

Now go back and summarize what you have taught by having the four persons show again the four original statements and then flip over to the solutions. This enables you to review the whole presentation; it also will fix the ideas more firmly in the minds of those listening.

This may seem like an overly simple presentation, but it is the real simplicity that enables you to focus on the very important message of one's being responsible for all one's actions, a concept too often contradicted by today's values.

34

Little Things Mean a Lot

(Widow's Mite, First Communion)

This homily was in response to the Gospel story of the Widow's Mite (see Mk 12:38-44; 31st Sunday of the Year, Cycle B). (Toward the end of this presentation, I will show you how it can be adapted very effectively for a First Communion homily.) You remember that Jesus makes the point that the poor widow who gave only a couple of coins to the Temple actually gave more than the rich man who gave more, since her gift was all she had and he gave from his surplus. The challenge, as always, was to apply this to the children so that they could grasp the meaning and apply it to themselves.

As you will see, the items I used to make my point were thought of by me. If you can find identical items, that's fine, but the *idea* is the core of the message. What you use to illustrate it will depend on your own imagination and the availability of certain props.

PROPS

- **Several Giant Bills** (i.e., paper money of varying amounts). These can be obtained in toy stores or novelty shops.
- **An Equally Large Wallet.** This can be an envelope (minus the flap) made of brown construction paper or brown poster board cut to the proper size, and stapled or glued on three sides to form a pouch or wallet. (Use the handy glue-stick kind of paste applicator available in any stationery store. It is good, clean, and economical.)
- **Two Extra-Large Coins.** These can also be found in novelty shops, or you can use two large candy coins covered with silver or gold foil. You could also make them by cutting out cardboard disks and covering them with foil. Whatever you use, these two "coins" should be in a small drawstring bag or even a small paper bag (sack). (*Note: By the way, you will find that wandering through toy stores and novelty*

shops with your mind wide open and your imagination in gear can lead you to a whole array of valuable props for use with children. Try it. You'll be surprised at what you find – or what you'll remember when you start brainstorming in search of a children's homily.)

- **A Children's Picture Puzzle.** The kind of puzzle to use is one that comes with its own frame to hold the pieces together. This self-contained frame is of great value when you are holding the puzzle up for all to see. I used one of Mickey and Minnie Mouse (the kids easily recognize them) and removed one of the pieces. A second children's puzzle showed the states of the United States. I removed the smallest piece, the one showing Connecticut, Massachusetts, and Rhode Island. A third one I have used is of Aladdin, from which I removed the piece showing his face.
- **A Single Altar Bread.**

HOMILY

Begin with the statement "Little things mean a lot" and begin to review the Gospel story. As you do, bring out the drawstring (or paper) bag containing the two coins. Remove the coins and show them to the children, explaining that these are the two coins that the widow gave. Place the coins on the altar and show that the bag is now empty. Place the bag next to the coins. Then show the wallet, and take out and show all the large bills – the larger the denomination the better! Now count out a couple of the bills and place them beside the two coins, pointing out the difference in value between the coins and the bills. Then count out the rest of the bills, clearly showing the children how much money the rich man still had in his wallet. Finally, state how the widow gave everything she had, and how the rich man gave *more* than she did, but that he had a whole lot left over, which he kept for himself. So, as Jesus says, the widow's gift was *worth* a lot more. "Little things mean a lot."

Now show the first puzzle. The children will quickly notice that a piece is missing. State that the puzzle is of little value until the lost piece is found. Produce it, set in place, and show that "little things mean a lot." Then take the other puzzle (the one with the 50 states) and show that the smallest piece is missing, so the puzzle is incomplete. Stating again that "little things mean a lot," fit the piece in place, and have the kids indicate that the puzzle is now complete (by applause, laughter, or whatever).

You might also remark to the adults that the smallest piece in the puzzle is also the only one that has three states on it; so, as small as it is, this piece is of great importance – especially to the inhabitants of those three states! This is a special message to the adults, too, who tend to judge the value of everything according to its size. Once again, "little things mean a lot." *(Examples of other items bearing this message are listed in another presentation of this message in Chapter 3, "Little Things Are Important," page 26.)*

Now ask them a question: "During this Mass, we are going to use something that is quite small, but which will become very, very special during the Mass. Can anyone tell me what that thing is?" You will be surprised at how soon one of the children will mention the host that they will receive in Holy Communion. Congratulate them and hold the host up, reminding them that in a few minutes this will be turned into *Jesus!* This is a wonderful example of how "little things mean a lot." This host, which costs only a penny or so, will soon become absolutely priceless!

Finally, since many of them will not be able to receive Holy Communion because of their age, point to *them* and indicate in whatever way you wish that even though *they* are little, they are very, very special, and that God considers each one of them to be His child. You can develop this as much as you like, putting the emphasis on how, even though they are little, they are of great importance to God and His Church. Among other reasons, that's why you have prepared these special talks every time you have a Family Mass!

Then, showing that you are a good teacher, review the whole talk briefly, using the props to recall that "little things mean a lot" – and so do little people!

The first time I used this homily, one of the ushers told me after Mass that one little girl went back to her seat with a big grin on her face and said to her mother, "See, Father Brennan says I'm special," and then, pointing to her mother said, "And Mommy, so are you!" What more positive feedback could a homilist want than that?

35

This Little Light of Mine and the Salt of the Earth

(Power of Good Example)

Obviously, this homily is our answer to the Gospel in which Jesus proclaims, "You are the salt of the earth. . . . You are the light of the world" (see Mt 5:13-16; Fifth Sunday of the Year, Cycle A).

The first part of that statement can be dealt with in a question-and-answer session without using graphics or props. A question-and-answer format by itself can be a real "attention getter and holder" if the questions are clearly asked and the answers responded to in short, precise comments. The main idea is to hold the children's attention so they will hear your message. This can be done with thoughtful questions and answers. This format can also give rise to some very surprising answers — but as we noted above, if you are relaxed and ready to accept the children's answers, whatever they may be, you may not only give an interesting and even humorous homily, but also endear yourself to the children for accepting them as they are.

*(Note: If I may inject another lesson from the world of magic, it is believed that the best form of misdirection — i.e., of directing someone's attention to where you want it and away from something you don't want them to see — is to ask them a direct question. In teaching, the same rule applies: Asking questions keeps focusing the children's attention in the direction you want to go, and if they are comfortable with you, they will want to be the ones to give the correct answer. It is also a fine way to keep **all** of the children involved. So attention will be no problem as long as the questions are clear and well planned.)*

('You are the salt of the earth.')

Begin by asking them what we use salt for. They probably have never thought about it, so give them a few moments to get their "thinking caps" on, and then wait for the answers. Here are the likely responses:

- **We use it to make things taste better.** Comment on how we can make things go better or feel better if we follow the teachings of Jesus. Doing things that will always please Jesus makes us feel good about ourselves and others.
- **We use it to melt snow.** We can use the Word of God and the teachings of Jesus to melt hard hearts. We can forgive others and be patient with them, and thus show them how Jesus loves them and how we love them, too — even if we don't *like* what they do. (Children should learn the difference between *liking* someone and *loving* them.)
- **We use it to preserve things.** You may have to "fish" for this answer, explaining how, before refrigerators and freezers, people preserved food by putting salt on it — that's why ham always tastes so salty! We can also keep our lives fresh and happy by doing what Jesus asks us to do and showing others how they can be happy.
- **We use it to purify things.** Talk about "pouring salt on a wound" to kill the germs that might gather there and cause an infection. Tell them that's what people did before they had iodine and Mercurochrome and bacitracin! Then explain how, by doing what Jesus did, we can keep from being bad and causing others pain (such as when we say or do mean things to them).
- **We use it to gargle and heal a sore throat.** This answer was given to me by one of the children — I wasn't prepared to hear this one! But if it is offered, pick up on it, and agree that doing God's work certainly makes us feel better and gets rid of any bad ideas we might have about disobeying, being mean, or telling lies.

I don't know of any more uses of salt that the children will give, so simply repeat these, sum things up, and bring the homily to a close.

If you wish to go on to the second part of the statement, then perhaps you can do it with the next offering.

PROPS
('You are the light of the world.')

- A 10" candle in a stand.
- An empty glass from a sanctuary-lamp candle.
- As many construction-paper candles as you need to have one for each child. These are simply made from a piece of red construction paper about 6" x 1" and a piece of yellow construction paper cut in the shape of a flame. The flame is pasted to the top of the candle. These should be given to some of the members of your helpers committee, to be given at the end of the homily or the end of the Mass.
- A box of matches or a lighter.

HOMILY
('You Are the Light of the World')

Ask the children what we use a lighted candle for. They will come up with several answers, among which might be:

- **We use it to give light.** We are called to brighten up the day for other people by being cheerful and helpful and good.
- **We use it to light our way.** Jesus wants us to be a light for others by showing them the way. Ask them to give several illustrations of giving good example.
- **We use light for heat.** How wonderful it is to have a fire on a cold night (especially for children who have fireplaces or who have gone camping). Give suggestions — or ask the children to give them — of how we can bring comfort to others, especially when they feel alone or sad.

Now comment on how Jesus asks us to be the light of the world for others. We are not to hide our light (or "put it under a bushel basket"). Show the children what happens when they do this (i.e., when they put their light under a basket or hide it so no one can see it). Light the candle, and then hold the sanctuary-lamp glass upside down and place it over the candle. In a few seconds it will consume the air in the glass and go out, but the children will be able to *see* this happen through the side of the glass. That's what happens when they do not use the light that Jesus gives them. His light in them goes out!

Bring the homily to a conclusion by teaching them the wonderful song "This Little Light of Mine." (Any grade school teacher or Scout leader can teach it to you if you don't know it.) If you really sing poorly, then have someone from the Music Ministry Committee lead the song; but if it is at all possible for *you* to lead it, do so. This carries far more impact and gives greater continuity to the whole presentation. It also delivers the very important, if somewhat subliminal, message that you don't have to have a great voice to sing in church! If you can carry a tune, that's all that matters.

Before singing the song, *go over the words with the children, verse by verse.* This will give the little ones a chance to learn and understand the words, and you will get lots of help in this teaching from the older children, who will almost certainly know this song.

Be sure that you use the usual hand gestures that go with each verse of the song, even if you don't sing. The children will enjoy doing them and seeing you do them, too, and the gestures are an excellent example of learning by doing (they are another form of visual art). The older ones will have the added fun of teaching the little ones not only the words, but also the gestures. *In short, get involved in what you want them to do.* Don't worry about how you look. The children will love it, and you might even reveal some of your human side to the grown-ups! And for heaven's sake, put a smile on your face!

If you want this homily to really work, then get the *adults* involved, too. Have them sing the song, *with the hand gestures,* and get everyone to *clap in rhythm* to the last verse. Yes, it's okay to clap in church, especially when you are singing about the joy that is yours because the Lord has called you to be His light in the world!

Finally, you can have your committee members give the construction-paper candles out to the children as they leave the sanctuary.

36

What We Want vs. What We Need

(Consumerism, Greed, Simple Life, Power of Possessions)

This is a favorite topic of mine with our children, who are so suscep-
tible to the powers of our consumer society. Thanks to the overload
of commercials and the example of celebrities, they almost always see
happiness as coming from the amount of things they own, and whether
these are the "latest, biggest, fastest, or most expensive."

This particular opportunity to deal with this situation arose on the
15th Sunday of the Year, Cycle B (see Mk 6:7-13), in the Gospel passage
wherein Jesus sends out the apostles and tells them what to take and
what not to take. This theme comes up in other Scripture passages, and
this is a simple way to deal with it. It takes little preparation of props,
involves all the children in the presentation, and delivers a very important lesson for our times.

PROPS

You will need a piece of poster board (22" x 14") fastened to something
stiff, like wood, thick cardboard, or foam core that will enable you to
write on the poster board while holding it erect. Of course, you could
also use newsprint on an easel, but this does not allow you to move
around as much, if that is your style of preaching to kids. You will also
need a broad-point felt-tip pen.

Before giving the homily, on one side of the poster board list all the
essential things you need for a specific part of life. Print the heading
"**THINGS NEEDED FOR . . .**" (At the summer camp, I listed those things
that the camp brochure said the boys needed to bring with them.) Depending on your circumstances, you might list those things you *need* in
a classroom, for some popular activity or sport they are all familiar with,
or perhaps ask them what they feel they need to be happy in their lives.
Write these on the front of the poster board.

Begin by having one of the children read aloud the list you have printed. Explain the source of your list. Now ask them what else they feel they need in the particular circumstance you have chosen. (At the camp, I asked the boys what else they had brought in their trunks.)

As the children call out the items, turn the poster board over and write their responses. Write these things in two columns so that you can get as many on the board as they give you. Don't be afraid to affirm whatever they call out, especially if it is unusual. Remember, these things are important to the *child*; that's what you asked for.

Now ask them to think about two different words: **NEED** and **WANT**. Explain the differences, emphasizing that they *cannot* get along without things they *need*, while they *can* get along without things they *want*, even though life can be more pleasant with those things. Tie all these things in with the question: "Will these things you *want* really make you happy for a long time?"

Then ask them to think back to the most recent Christmas and to try to recall what they wanted most to receive as a gift. (Some of them won't even be able to remember, which makes your point right away, but don't comment on this here. Wait until later in the homily.) Surely they thought that if only they got what they wanted, they would be the happiest kid in town; they really *needed* that gift to be happy. But later that Christmas Day, when they went to visit some relatives or friends and saw what *they* got for Christmas, how quickly they changed their mind and now they wanted what the relatives or friends had! So what we *want* is very often *not* something we *need*!

Now go over the list of things they added to your original list and ask about each one of them: "Do you *need* this or do you just *want* it?" Mark each item "N" or "W." Indicate through this list how few (if any) of the things they added they really *need*. Then go back to the Gospel and show how Jesus instructed His apostles about how little they needed for their journey of spreading the Word of God. Help the children to see that the only thing the apostles really *needed* was their faith in what Jesus had told them, to share with those who would listen. Finally, you should be able to conclude by stating that the only thing we *really need* in life is Jesus!

This would be a fine time to say something about the consumerism that has led to so much excess in our nation. We buy according to labels, styles, models, and fads. It is reflected in the expression "He who dies with the most toys wins." I recently heard a variation on that expression that says, "He who dies with the most toys still dies!" Now *that's* a message many of us, children and adults, need to hear.

37

Our Most Precious Gift

(Our Catholic Faith)

The idea for this homily came from the use of what cartoonists call "balloons" — i.e., the bubble-like areas in which the cartoonist prints the words the characters in the cartoon are supposed to be speaking. It is another use of signs, but in a different form, and it grabs the kids' attention because you use one of them to hold each sign. You also involve the entire group in trying to determine what the contents of each balloon might be.

The point of the homily is to impress upon the children that, more than anything else they may have, their most precious gift is their Catholic faith. If you ask them what the most important things in their lives are, you will get a series of answers — not entirely unexpected (I hope). And those answers will reflect those things the kids really think are most important. After all, they are children! Their mature set of values is only beginning to be developed. The purpose of this homily is to lead them to begin to understand that their *Catholic faith* is the most precious gift of all.

PROPS

You will need a set of signs, on each of which is printed one of the things most children think are important. If possible, each of these should be printed on a different color poster board and using different type styles for the printing. (Here's where you call again on that wonderful parishioner who is your volunteer artist!) Then the poster board should be cut to 22" x 14", except for the last one which should be a full size (22" x 28"). Most importantly, all of these signs — except the last one — should be cut to an oval shape with a small fin-like appendage, just as you see in cartoons. The fin-like piece shows which character the thought is coming from. (See illustration.) As noted above, the last one (Catholic faith) should be on a full-size poster board. This need not be cut into the balloon shape.

The words on the signs could be any of the following, or whatever "most important things" you feel are appropriate for the age level to whom you are speaking. I first did this for some middle-school children, so I figured that the most important things for them were **SPORTS**, **FRIENDS**, **PASSING GRADES**, **TOYS**, **MONEY**, and **CARS** (especially if there are lot of boys present). Other topics could have been the **LATEST STYLES**, **MY COMPUTER**, **MY PET(S)**, **TV**, etc. You will know from the age group you are dealing with what the topics probably will be. But if you need help in determining these, ask either the children's teachers or their parents. You'll get lots of sound ideas.

HOMILY

Before beginning the homily, call forward as many children as you have "balloon" signs prepared. Keep the last one (**MY CATHOLIC FAITH**) for yourself. Give one sign to each child, but ask them to keep the signs down in front of themselves, with the printing facing them, not facing the other children. Instruct them also to have the fin-like appendage facing upward so that, when they hold the sign over their head, the fin will now be on the bottom and indicate that the thought is coming from the child holding the sign.

Begin the homily by asking the children to take a few moments and think about the most important possession they have or (in the case of teenagers) will have. After "priming the pump" by offering some suggestions (*not* all those on the balloon signs) to get them started, give them a minute or two to think about it. Then ask them to raise their hands (don't let them simply call out). Call on the ones who you think will have the best answers. (Be prepared for some "surprises"!) If you have prepared a half-dozen or more balloon signs, you should have among them most of the things the young people will name.

After the youngsters have told you what their "most prized possessions" are, direct their attention to the children up front who are holding the balloon signs. Point to the first one, and have the child holding it raise it up over his/her head. Point to it and talk about it. Then ask the one holding it if that really is his/her most prized possession. (After all, you simply handed the sign to them when they came forward. They didn't select it!) If one of the kids in the larger group has already named that prized possession, then ask him/her to explain why that was the choice. Then go on to the next balloon sign, and continue until you have finished.

When all the balloons have been shown and commented on, the chances are that no one will have thought of "MY CATHOLIC FAITH" because they either don't see that as prized or they don't see it as a possession. That's when you hold up your sign and speak to them about what is truly their most prized possession. At no time should you criticize them for not having thought of it — after all, it is a rather mature concept — but encourage them to think about what a wonderful gift it is. It helps them to know God (Father, Son, and Holy Spirit), the Blessed Mother, and their patron saint; it brings the Bible into their lives; it helps them to pray; it's what makes it possible for them to receive baptism, have their sins forgiven through reconciliation, and receive Jesus in the Eucharist, and so on. These are things that the little ones rarely think about, and they might not even think about them for too long after you name them. But it's never too late to get them to begin to grow in their understanding of how precious a gift their Catholic faith is.

Conclude by pointing to the balloon signs again, by showing how the things they now prize are passing things that will not last too long, and how they will have their Catholic faith for the rest of their lives as long as they prize it and use it.

Should a child give you a response that is *not* on one of the balloon signs, affirm them in their choice by asking why they feel this is so important. After all, you asked them what their most prized possession is, so their answer can't be wrong. Also, by indicating the variety of answers, you show that everyone will have different items they prize, since God gives us different gifts as well as different interests and hobbies. And besides, you couldn't possibly think of them all!

38

The Workers in the Vineyard

(God's Grace, One's Individuality, Gifts and Talents)

Rather than try to explain this parable (see Mt 20:1-16; 25th Sunday of the Year, Cycle A) to children in terms of fairness — a task that is daunting enough with adults — I would speak about the enormous generosity of God to all who are open to His grace. I define grace as "God living in and through us." The point of this homily, then, is to show that, while each of us is different in many ways, especially in the gifts and talents we receive from God, He gives each of us all that we need to do His will each day. He has a special plan for each of us, and so He gives us all we need to fulfill that plan.

PROPS

- Four clear drinking glasses, *each a different size and shape.* (Mine are plastic to avoid breakage in case of an accident. A trip to a good housewares or kitchenware store should supply these.)
- Two or three drops of food dye in the bottom of each glass — i.e., a different color in each glass. This is food dye that is found in the grocery store in the baking section; it is used to make different colors of icing. It usually comes in four colors.
- A clear pitcher with water sufficient in amount to almost fill all the glasses. This should have a label reading "**GRACE**" on the side.
- A tray on which to place the glasses and pitcher, so that all these can be easily removed at the end of the homily.

HOMILY

Speak about how different we all are: size, skin color, abilities, national origin, etc. "All these go together to make us special and unique, one-of-a-kind individuals," you will say. "God has never made anyone quite like me — or you. He gives each of us different gifts and talents, too." *(Name some of these, being careful not to stress sports or performing skills.)*

"He also created each of us to play a part in the whole story of the world, a part that no others can play because they are not us! But God does not leave us alone to do our part. He gives us a special gift called *grace*. When we receive grace, it means we have God's life, God's power within us. He gives us the help and energy to do what He created us to do. He gives us all we need, and it is different in each of us because He made us different from each other. Let me show you what I mean." *(Bring out the tray with the four glasses and the water pitcher.)*

"Each of the glasses is different, just as we are. *(Show each glass, and point out the differences — size, shape, stem, no stem, etc.)* At our baptism, we receive grace — God's life — for the first time. God continues to give us grace every day of our lives. He also gives us different talents and gifts. Let's see how it works."

(Hold up the pitcher.) "This pitcher is filled with water, which stands for God's gift of *grace*. Notice that this first glass is different in size and shape from the others. *(Pour water into the first glass. The children will notice it changes color.)* Notice how the 'grace' changes the color. That's because God's grace works differently in each one of us. Perhaps this person has the grace of patience and the gift to draw or paint."

(Point out the difference in shape and size of the second glass. Pour water into the second glass. The children will see how the "grace" is a different color from the first.) "Perhaps this person has the grace of joy and fun, as well as the gift of making music with his or her voice or an instrument."

(Continue with the remaining glasses, pointing out their differences in size and shape, and then pour the water and cite such graces as strong faith, peacefulness, generosity, forgiveness, courage, etc. and such gifts as athletic ability, facility with languages, mechanical skills, being good at certain subjects in school, etc., making your examples age-appropriate and in terms the children can understand.)

"So you see how generous God is to all of us. He gives us special graces and gifts so we can become the persons He wants us to be. We should pray every day to know our graces and gifts. We should *not* keep asking for gifts other people have! God knows what He wants each of us to do with our lives, and He will give us all we need to do that. It is up to each of us now to discover and then use these gifts and graces the way God wants us to. In that way, God will be happy and we will be happy because we will become the person God wants us to be, and not somebody else."

An Afterthought

This homily resulted from an annual workshop I give on homilies for kids to the deacons at our seminary who are preparing for ordination to the priesthood. After showing them what I have done, I give the seminarians four Gospel readings, or other readings, and ask them to do some brainstorming so as to awaken their own imaginations. (Indeed, that is the real purpose of this book: to get you to use *your* imagination, too!)

The idea of the different glasses came from one of the seminarians. But pouring plain water into all of them served only to show our differences; it did not clearly show that God's grace is different in each of us. So we came up with the idea of having the water turn a different color in each glass. That's what brainstorming (and prayer) can do! The water changing colors also fascinates the children (and those adults who are paying attention!) and holds their interest throughout.

A Final Thought

Since the point of this homily is to establish the uniqueness of each of us — and we have done that by the different shapes and sizes of the glasses as well as the different-colored water in each — you might conclude by asking: "Suppose God made us all the same, without our special gifts and graces — how would we all look? (*Then pour the water from each glass back into the pitcher. The liquid will turn murky and dark.*) Surely, this is not how God wants us all to look!"

39

The Failure of the Sower

(Encouragement, Growth, How We Succeed)

The parable of the Sower in Matthew's Gospel (see Mt 13:1-23; 15th Sunday of the Year, Cycle A) is one of the few that carries its own explanation. Whether you feel that it is really the explanation offered by Jesus or was added by a member of Matthew's community matters little in this context. What is obvious is that the parable is quite well explained in the verses that follow the telling of the parable, and it would be well to leave that explanation alone, especially where children are concerned. So what do we do with this very popular Gospel at a Mass for children?

We look for some other aspect of the story that will apply to children, and I think one of those can be our *fear of failure*. For you see, reading through the parable, we can conclude that the sower was successful in scattering the seed only 25 percent of the time, or one time out of every four! That's not a very good percentage in any undertaking — but it is good enough for God!

Another way to look at this is to see that the sower *failed* three times out of four; but once that fourth part was complete, it brought about great results: thirty-fold, sixty-fold, and a hundred-fold. We can point to Jesus' crucifixion as a colossal failure — for three days — and then state that the success of His life was brought about by His being raised from the dead by the Father. Jesus failed to win over the Pharisees and tax collectors. He failed in his self-defense before Pilate and Herod. And He initially failed to instill courage in the hearts and wills of the apostles. It was only after the Resurrection — the ultimate sign of our salvation — that His life was clearly identified as a life dedicated to fidelity to the Father's will, a sure guarantee of eternal success.

The point of this homily for children, then, is to lead them to understand that it is all right to fail, as long as we do our very best and try to do even better the next time. The Lord asks us to *try*, and not necessarily to succeed — or to quote Mother Teresa, "Jesus doesn't ask us to be successful, but to be faithful."

You will provide a series of illustrations showing failure and then true success, based on examples that are appropriate to the children you are addressing. You could have an artistically inclined parishioner create the illustrations or simply draw them with stick figures. The illustrations I use are those employed at summer camp Mass, where the mix of English-speaking and Spanish-speaking boys was about equal; yours will be different according to the makeup of the assembly. All illustrations are done on pieces of 14" x 22" poster board.

1. A sign that reads: **(a) WE <u>FAIL</u>, (b) WE <u>LISTEN</u>, (c) WE <u>LEARN</u>, (d) WE <u>GROW</u>**.
2. A picture of a boy or girl swinging at a pitched baseball — and missing. The reverse shows the same person hitting a home run!
3. A picture of a target with arrows flying by it or sticking out of the ground in front of it. The reverse shows several arrows hitting the target, with one or two in the bull's-eye.
4. A picture of a sailboat "hung in irons" (with the sails hanging loosely, so the boat is not moving). The reverse shows the same boat with the sail full and sailing along nicely.
5. A picture of a poor drawing of Mickey Mouse. The reverse shows a fine drawing of Mickey Mouse.
6. A sign that says, "**SPANISH: How do you say, <u>How old are you?</u>**" Underneath are the words, "**¿Cómo viejo eres?**" This is a *literal* translation of the words *How* (Cómo) *old* (viejo) *are you* (eres). The reverse shows the same question — "**SPANISH: How do you say, How old are you?**" — and the answer in the *correct* Spanish idiom — "**¿Cuántos años tienes?**" (which literally means "How many years do you have?").
7. A sign that says, "**ENGLISH: How do you pronounce OUGH?**" The reverse shows "**BOUGH – ow**"; "**TOUGH – uff**"; "**THOUGH – owe**"; "**THOUGHT – awe**"; and "**THROUGH – ooo.**"
8. A sign that says:

   WE <u>FAIL</u> WHEN WE:
   DISOBEY
   LIE

STEAL
CHEAT
DON'T SHARE
CURSE
MAKE FUN OF OTHERS

The reverse side of the sign says:

WE GROW WHEN WE:
  OBEY
  TELL THE TRUTH
  ASK TO BORROW
  PLAY FAIR
  SHARE WITH OTHERS
  CONTROL OUR TONGUE
  ARE KIND TO OTHERS

These cards should be in order as listed, with the *failure* side shown first, then turned around to show the *success* side.

HOMILY

From all the above, it should be clear how this homily is structured. You begin by telling the children how Jesus, the farmer, spread the seed, but *only one seed out of every four actually grew.* If you wish, you can also make reference to the Crucifixion as something that looked like a *failure*, but actually was a *success*, when three days later Jesus rose again.

You might say, "We fail in many things we try to do for the first time. But failing is not something to be embarrassed about unless we do not *learn* from the failure. Let's look at some examples."

This is where you use the posters, which are quite self-explanatory, although you should comment on each of them for maximum clarification. As you go through the examples, keep repeating the four steps: we *fail,* we *listen* (to our parents, teachers, priests, coaches, etc.), we *learn,* and then (when we get it right) we *grow.* "So just as Jesus had only one out of four seeds bear fruit," you might say, to wrap things up, "so we can fail at things we do the first time (or even the second or third time). But if we are willing to listen and learn, we will grow in our ability to do things well, one step at a time — both in our everyday activities and, most importantly, in our spiritual lives."

This lesson can be phrased, and the illustrations can be drawn, to fit the age group — but the lesson is one that can be taught to people of *all* ages. This is just one more time when the lesson, ostensibly taught to the children, can also be learned by the adults.

40

It's a Jumble Out There!

(Multipurpose Teaching Device)

Every morning I enjoy my muffin and milk while reading the newspaper. On the comic pages there is a puzzle called "The Jumble," which I try to do in my head (i.e., without writing in the answers). It consists of four words, the letters of which are scrambled (e.g., "water" might be written as "trawe"). As you fill in the correct answer, one or two of the letters will be placed in a box containing a circle. For the solution of the jumble, you have to unscramble all the letters in the circles.

It occurred to me one morning that this would be a fun way to teach a lesson in a homily. Kids love to solve puzzles, and the method of the jumble assures that they will pay attention right through, until the end of the homily.

PROPS

You will need some poster board, three different-colored felt-tipped markers (I suggest black, green, and red), and a ruler. Use the black marker to draw the boxes in which you will write the letters that are **not** part of the final answer. The boxes should be at least 4" square. Use the red marker to make the boxes in which you will write the letters that will form the final answer (instead of using a circle in the box, which the newspaper uses but which diminishes the space you have for printing the letters.) Use the green marker for printing the letters in the boxes.

After experimenting with several methods, I arrived at what I feel is the easiest and most effective way to use the jumble for homily purposes. For each word that you are going to unscramble, cut a piece of white poster board 6" high and as long as it needs to be in order to accommodate the proper number of boxes (one for each letter). Now draw the required number of boxes on the card. The boxes should be at least four inches square so as to be easily seen by all. Remember that the boxes that contain letters that are *not* part of the final answer should be black. The boxes that contain the letters that *are* part of the final answer should be red.

On one side of the card, print the scrambled word. Then flip the card over and draw the appropriate boxes on that side. In those boxes print the letters of the *unscrambled* word. Do this for as many words as you have chosen to produce the final answer. Because everything is now preprinted, this method eliminates your having to do any printing while you are presenting the homily.

Obtain a piece of foam core of sufficient size to accommodate the four or five cards you have prepared. Arrange sufficient pushpins on the board so that you can rest the cards on them, two or three pins for each card. Since the cards are 6" high, the rows of pins should be at least 6 1/2" apart. Resist the urge to put all the cards on the board at the beginning. Holding back will not only build suspense but will also prevent the brighter children from going ahead of the rest. Should the final answer contain two or more words — depending on the age of the children participating — you might want to group the letters from the first answers according to the number and order of words in the final answer.

When you begin, then, you should have resting on an easel the foam core piece in which you will have inserted sufficient pushpins on which to rest the prepared word cards. The cards themselves should be located on a table or on the altar so as not to be seen until you hold them up, one at a time. The large piece of poster board that contains the final answer should be under the other pieces. As mentioned above, the scrambled letters from which the final answer will result should be preprinted on the final card. Simply state when you show it to the children that the letters you are showing them are all the ones taken from the *red* boxes. On the reverse side of the final-answer card, you will preprint that answer, the *unscrambled* word(s).

Throughout the homily, comment on each of the words as it is unscrambled. Then group the letters in the red boxes. To conclude, unscramble these letters, arrive at the final answer, and make your closing comments. Good teaching style will lead you to review each of the words and the final answer to drive your point home.

The challenge for you is to find four or five words that fit your theme and also contain the letters you need to produce the final answer, which is also the main message you want to convey. Let me give you two or three examples.

The first time I used this method was at the Parish School Mass, at which the eighth-graders received their school pins. So I chose five words because I needed that many words to provide the letters for the final answer. The words were **ALTOLYY**, **CRIVEES**, **SHINOLES**, **PHAYP**, and **ERPID**. The unscrambled words were **LOYALTY**, **SERVICE**, **HOLINESS**, **HAPPY**, and **PRIDE**. (See illustration.) The letters that are underlined were the ones written in the red boxes and used in the final answer.

Preprinted on the final-answer card, the scrambled letters for the final answer were **LOSCHONSSPPI**; when they were unscrambled, the final answer was **SPS** (St. Patrick's School) **SCHOOL PIN**. (I helped them with the SPS part.)

At the Marist Brothers Camp, on the occasion of the annual celebration of the solemn profession of many of the Brothers (July 26), I used the scrambled words **SOPSIMER**, **SATTICHY**, **VOTEPRY**, **BICEODEEN**, and **TRESCEP**. The unscrambled words were **PROMISES**, **CHASTITY**, **POVERTY**, **OBEDIENCE**, and **RESPECT**. Again, the letters that are underlined are the ones used in the final answer, in this case giving two words (preprinted on the separate poster board). The

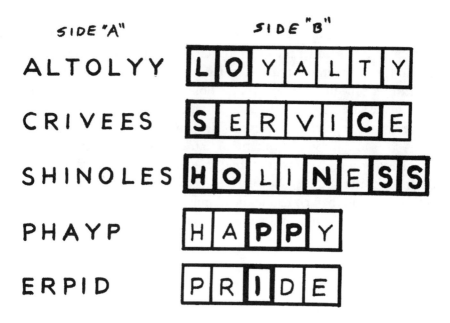

SIDE "A"   SIDE "B"

ALTOLYY   LOYALTY

CRIVEES   SERVICE

SHINOLES   HOLINESS

PHAYP   HAPPY

ERPID   PRIDE

two scrambled words were **RIMSAT** and **ORTHREB**, and they were unscrambled as **MARIST BROTHER**.

Here is a third example: **VIRASO, ESSUJ, PHESDRESH, HELMBEETH, RAYM,** and **ROLACS**. When these words were unscrambled, they were **SAVIOR, JESUS, SHEPHERDS, BETHLEHEM, MARY,** and **CAROLS**, all things that have to do with Christmas. Again, the underlined letters provide two words: **RERYM** and **SAMTHIRCS**. When unscrambled, the words were **MERRY CHRISTMAS**.

HOMILY

Actually, most of the work is done in the preparation. Set the cards in order so that each scrambled word is face-up. Introduce the idea of the homily and that you are going to ask them to solve a puzzle to find the idea. Now show them the first card with its unscrambled word. Wait for them to unscramble it, and then flip the card over, showing the correct answer. Point out that some of the letters are in red boxes. Tell them that these will be used to find the final answer. Place this card on the large foam core on the easel so that it rests on the two or three pushpins, which serve as a kind of wall bracket. Do the same with the rest of the word cards.

When you have finished with the four or five word cards, they should be displayed one under the other, resting on the pushpins. Now point out all the letters in the red boxes. These will be used to arrive at the final answer, the main message of the homily. Hold up the final-answer card (make sure it's the *scrambled* side), and show how all the letters in the red boxes are now on this card. (Here you can remove the previous cards so as to call complete attention to the scrambled message on the final-answer card.) Now ask the children to solve the puzzle. When they do, then flip the card over showing the unscrambled message, make your comments, and then conclude the homily, remembering to review the four or five word cards and showing again how they led to the final-answer card.

Some Thoughts About Puppets

(Wonderful Device When Used Well)

While I would never refer to myself as a puppet master, I have had some experience with the little critters and recommend them to you as another fine visual and animated device for reaching out to the children.

Puppets are not hard to manipulate. Place your forefinger into the head, and your thumb and ring finger (or little finger) into the two arms, and you are ready to go. That's if you are using puppets with arms. You may have to use different digits depending on the puppet you are using.

There has been a resurgence in the popularity of puppets, and there are some beautiful ones on the market. In addition to the "people" puppets, I also have a crocodile ("Lyle"), whose teeth are made of a white zipper; an owl ("Socrates"), whose wings flap and whose head turns 360 degrees; and a lion and rabbit. I have also seen a praying mantis, a spider, a skunk, a squirrel, and sundry other wonderful creatures that you could build delightful stories around. Some of them are a bit expensive, but the old expression — "You get what you pay for" — applies. My suggestion is to purchase good puppets but, before you buy any, have some idea as to how you will use them. You don't want to buy them, use them once, and then have them sit on a shelf.

The puppet ought to be introduced to the children in a special way. For example, the puppet could be in a bag (a gift bag would be fine, the size determined by the size of the puppet or the occasion for its use) and appear over the top edge of the bag. This is simply done by cutting a hole in the back of the bag (the side away from the audience), inserting your hand through the hole and into the puppet, and then showing the puppet over the front edge of the bag. It could also be in a box with a lid on it. The arrangement could be the same as with the bag, with the puppet being shown looking over the edge of the box after the top is removed.

The only problem with the above method is that it leaves you working the puppet with the bag or box still on your arm. The simplest solution to that problem would be to cut a slot in the back of the bag or the side of the box (instead of just a hole), which would allow you to slip the bag or box off your arm once you have slipped your hand into the puppet and the puppet has been introduced.

As for giving the puppet a voice, there are two ways to do it. Either you provide the voice or someone else does. In the first instance, you do not have to be a ventriloquist, but you should try to develop some voice that sounds different from yours. Otherwise, you will be confusing your listeners as to exactly who is speaking. As long as you make that difference, you need not try to conceal the fact that the voice is coming from you. Of course, if you can do that, so much the better.

The other way to give your puppet a voice is to use your church sound system. Plug an extra microphone into the amplifier and have someone else provide the voice. This provides a totally different sound for the puppet, relieves you of having to "think" for both you and the puppet, and allows you to concentrate on having the puppet's movements coincide with what it is "saying." (The first time I did this at a Family Mass, I got rave reviews on what a brilliant ventriloquist I was!) The only difficulty with this method is that your presentation has to be scripted so that you and the person providing the puppet's voice are literally "on the same page." This requires that you memorize the script. You could work around this by having your homily presented as something you are reading to the puppet from a book, with the puppet making occasional comments, asking questions, etc. This removes the need for memorizing the script.

Finally, one of the mistakes I have made is to write a script that involved myself and the puppet in conversation, a conversation that carried the message I wanted to deliver but which did *not* include the children. It was not long before they lost interest. So be sure that your presentation includes questions or actual dialogue addressed to those who are listening. In this way, they feel they are part of the homily, will stay interested in what you and the puppet are saying, and will come away with the message you want to deliver.

All the above presumes that you will be manipulating the puppet and either providing the voice or having someone else do that. The alternative would be for you to have a screen built, behind which you would have someone else manipulate the puppet. This could be as simple or ornate as you wish it to be, but a simple three-sided screen will focus the attention on the puppet(s) and you. This manner of presentation also removes from you the need to manipulate the puppet. The voices can easily be provided by those manipulating the puppets. Just put a microphone behind the screen.

One of the things that will bring your puppets "alive" is for you to regard them as another *person* with whom you are carrying on a conversation. It is not a toy on your other hand; it is a person with a personality. Therefore, you should always speak to it as if you actually are speaking to another person, and react to what it says. Moreover, you should be sure that it reacts to what *you* are saying. This can be done simply by controlling the direction in which the puppet is looking, a droop of its head, a sudden "take" by the puppet so it acts in a manner that reveals surprise or shock at what you say, and so on. What makes puppetry work is the illusion that the little doll (or animal) is actually alive, speaking with you, and reacting to what you are saying. You, too, must speak to it and react to what it is saying or doing. It is in this interaction between you and the puppet that the illusion is created that you are two people, not a person with a toy.

The last caution should be quite obvious by now. All of this requires rehearsal if it is to be done effectively. So sit and plan what you will do, write the script, obtain the puppets you will need, recruit your helpers (older kids love to do this kind of thing), and schedule a rehearsal. With all of this done well, you are ready to present what will be a memorable homily that will both teach and entertain.

Topical Index

About the Author

Msgr. Dermot R. Brennan was born on Manhattan's West Side, attended Corpus Christi Grammar School, Cathedral College, and was ordained from St. Joseph's Seminary, Dunwoodie, in 1956. He taught in the archdiocesan high schools for 12 years, during which he obtained a master's degree in music education from Teachers College, Columbia University. He served as chairman of the Archdiocesan Music Commission from 1969-1982, and conducted the chorus and orchestra at the Papal Mass at Yankee Stadium on October 4, 1979. He has been in parish work since 1970 and is currently pastor of the 4,500 households that make up St. Patrick's Parish in Yorktown Heights, New York. Msgr. Brennan's hobbies are music and performing magic.

Our Sunday Visitor . . .
Your Source for Discovering the Riches of the Catholic Faith

Our Sunday Visitor has an extensive line of materials for young children, teens, and adults. Our books, Bibles, booklets, CD-ROMs, audios, and videos are available in bookstores worldwide.

To receive a FREE full-line catalog or for more information, call **Our Sunday Visitor** at **1-800-348-2440**. Or write, **Our Sunday Visitor** / 200 Noll Plaza / Huntington, IN 46750.

- -

Please send me: __A catalog
Please send me materials on:
__Apologetics and catechetics   __Reference works
__Prayer books   __Heritage and the saints
__The family   __The parish

Name_____
Address_____Apt._____
City_____State____Zip_____
Telephone (   ) _____
                                              A23BBABP

- -

Please send a friend: __A catalog
Please send a friend materials on:
__Apologetics and catechetics   __Reference works
__Prayer books   __Heritage and the saints
__The family   __The parish

Name_____
Address_____Apt._____
City_____State____Zip_____
Telephone (   ) _____
                                              A23BBABP

- -

Our Sunday Visitor
200 Noll Plaza
Huntington, IN 46750
Toll free: **1-800-348-2440**
E-mail: osvbooks@osv.com
Website: www.osv.com